D0294879

N S

A SPECK IN THE SKY

A SPECK IN THE SKY

PETER MORAN, TD

ILLUSTRATED BY JOHN BATCHELOR

BLANDFORD PRESS
POOLE · NEW YORK · SYDNEY

First published in the UK 1987 by Blandford Press
Link House, West Street, Poole, Dorset BH15 1LL

Distributed in the United States by
Sterling Publishing Co, Inc,
2 Park Avenue, New York, NY 10016

Distributed in Australia by
Capricorn Link (Australia) Pty Ltd
PO Box 665, Lane Cove, NSW 2066

British Library Cataloguing in Publication Data

Moran, Peter
  A speck in the sky.
  1. Parachuting
  I. Title
  797.5'6'0924   GV770

ISBN 0 7137 1902 8

Typeset by August Filmsetting Ltd, Haydock, St Helens

Printed in Great Britain by
Garden City Press, Letchworth, Herts.

CONTENTS

To all those instructors who so patiently explained
the techniques of parachuting and gliding to me — thank you.

1

A SPECK IN THE SKY

A mile up in the sky there was a tiny speck. The speck was a man. His arms and legs were spreadeagled and he was lying face down on the air. Apart from the rapidly receding aeroplane from which he had jumped, he was alone in the sky. No other living creature, neither bird nor beast nor insect, was near him. His was the solitude of the only man in the vastness of the sky. It was a solitude made up of rushing air, wind noise and ruffling overalls, a vast emptiness of sky, some high-flying clouds and a remote earth. In the distance, far into the vast expanse of the horizon, was a gentle haze, an imperceptible blending of the rim of the earth and the dome of the sky. For the man it was an aloneness, not a loneliness, just a being alone somewhere between the sky and the earth. The man was me.

I had dropped now for three seconds in a stable spread. My arms and legs were comfortably spread out, my back was arched hollow, my head up. I held this position while my airspeed increased to 120 mph, nearly 180 feet every second, and the resistance of the air hardened. Then I gently inclined my head and shoulders to the right and rotated in a slow, elegant, lazy turn until I was again facing in my original direction. Eight seconds gone. For five of those seconds I had slowly rotated and surveyed the horizon around a complete circle. With a small contra-movement I stopped the turn. I decided to spend the next seven precious seconds in just being there, no manoeuvres, just being up there in the sky. So I lay there, a rapidly falling speck in an English summer sky dropping down towards a green English landscape.

If I had been asked, "Do you feel like a bird as you fly down through the air?" I might have replied, "No, I feel like a man flying. Man has always wanted to fly. He has used many means. He has flown with man-carrying kites, with gliders, with powered aeroplanes and with rockets. He has used balloons and airships and helicopters. I use my body. My control surfaces are my arms and my legs. My brain provides instrumentation, navigation and control, and all the pleasure, exhilaration, excitement and ecstasy of a man alone in the sky. For these few seconds, for this tiny slice of my life, I am not as other men, earthbound or sitting in mechanical flying machines. For these precious moments I am alone in the sky, without mechanical aids, indulging in the purest form of flying. These few seconds will remain within me for the rest of my life."

I might have replied like that, but more likely I would not, lest you think me foolish or a romantic. Or, perhaps like so many parachutists, I would be inarticulate when it came to giving verbal expression to my own deeply personal feelings about free fall. Or I might have replied with silence and a smile that told you nothing, except that whatever it was that I had experienced up there in the sky, it had been pleasurable.

For you can't put that sort of thing into words. The physical events can be described, but that is all. The other side of it, the mental, the spiritual side of the experience, can never be adequately described. It is something too deeply personal and unique to each of us. To each parachutist it is probably something quite different yet with the common thread of something out of this world, the ultimate which that person can conceive of. Is it the physical expression of the seeking after an ideal? A striving for perfection of technique? A modern, aerodynamic form of the quest for the Holy Grail? We would all like to express it, whatever it is, this being alone in the sky high above the green, detached, other worldly earth. But we can't, so we each hug to ourselves our own wordless experience of the ultimate, a personal treasure that only each one of us can fully appreciate. To find the treasure you must look for it alone, high in the sky in the vast space above the ground.

2

TRAINING WITH THE PARAS

Before you can seek the treasure you must first be trained as a parachutist. Then you must progress to become a free-fall parachutist. I trained as a military parachutist when I joined the Parachute Regiment (Territorial Army) in 1950.

I had previously spent three and a half undistinguished years in the army, mostly in India, during and after the war. After my demob I swore that I would not even join a Christmas Club. Then one day I was invited by a friend to visit his Territorial Army anti-aircraft unit at Childwall on the outskirts of Liverpool. "You would enjoy the TA," he told me. I agreed to come along and see what it was all about. So one Tuesday evening I crossed the Mersey by ferry boat from my home in Birkenhead to Liverpool. I saw the bus that would take me to Childwall and my friend's TA unit. Yet I walked past it, past the famous Liver Building, and onto the old Overhead Railway with its Victorian railway stations and carriages with decorative ceilings. The train took me out to Seaforth. I walked into Seaforth Barracks and announced, "I want to join the Parachute Regiment."

"Wait here," ordered the Regimental Sergeant-Major, a tall, bulky man. Half an hour later I was shown into the second-in-command's office. Another bulky man, he glowered at me and demanded, "Why do you want to join the Parachute Regiment?"

"Well, Sir . . ." I began. Then I stopped. For the life of me I didn't know what impulse had taken me to Seaforth instead of Childwall that evening. It was the start of sixteen years as a military parachutist in the TA.

I was sent to No. 1 Parachute Training School at RAF Abingdon (motto: "Knowledge Dispels Fear") to learn the skills and discipline of military parachuting. The ground training hangar contained all sorts of synthetic training equipment: slides, platforms for jumping off, harnesses slung from the roof, simulated fuselages, gym mats and the pièce de résistance, the fan. The dreaded fan! Many a would-be parachutist has changed his mind at the fan.

It consisted of a gallery high up in the hangar roof, perhaps thirty or forty feet above floor level. In the gallery there were openings to simulate the exit doors of aircraft. Above each opening was a pulley. Over the pulley passed a thin steel cable. The lower end of the cable, which reached down to the floor, terminated in a parachute harness. The upper end of the cable was wound round a drum attached to a fan. The end of the cable with the harness attached to it was wound up to the exit opening in the gallery. Here it was fitted to the would-be parachutist who then jumped out of the gallery onto a mat on the hangar floor forty feet below. As he fell, the cable round the drum would pay out and turn the drum and its attached fan. The air resistance on the fan would slow the jumper's rate of descent to about that of a parachute.

To reach the gallery with its exit doors we had to climb up a steel-runged ladder to the roof of the hangar, and step off it into the gallery. Climbing that awful ladder was the hardest thing I had to do in parachute training. It went up and up for ever! The higher I climbed the more slippery the rungs seemed to become. My hands sweated. Each step was an effort of will-power.

Somehow I reached the top where I stood on the wooden floor of the gallery wearing the harness. The instructor at my side ordered, "Stand to the door" and I took a pace forwards right into the door exit, the leading boot toecap just over the edge of the door, as I had been taught. "Look up, straight ahead of you!" Then a barked "Go!" and I leaped out into thin air as far as I could go. The cable, fan and gravity did the rest.

It was here that the first refusals, if there were to be any, would come. Anyone who refused found himself at Abingdon railway station within the hour, awaiting his train home. Refusals in parachuting are infectious, and in military activities refusals cannot be tolerated. One has a very deep sympathy for a man who refuses. Only another parachutist can even dimly imagine the mental agony of the man who, having spent hours or even days contemplating this thing that he is required to do, then decides that he is not the man he thought he was. He makes the irrevocable decision to speak his refusal – which in itself takes courage – and accepts his expulsion from the unit and the achievement he had hoped for. In the Regular Army parachuting refusals by qualified parachutists are severely treated with up to 112 days in a military prison (or were in those days). This is a quite correct and justifiable matter of military discipline. But every other military parachutist knows that it is a case of "There but for the Grace of God go I" and as a man, as distinct from being a soldier, will never condemn another man who refuses to parachute.

No man who has jumped off the fan will ever forget it. When the Parachute Regiment has a display stand at a military display and erects a fan on scaffolding, one can see all the children queuing to climb up and jump off this awesome training device. Then they go back for more! What happens to us between childhood and manhood to make us craven?

Outside the ground training hangar there were other training devices: a seventy-foot high platform below a massive boom, a pulley and wire, and of course the balloon.

The platform was noted for the energy needed to climb up all the steps in its steel structure. At the top the budding parachutist donned a harness attached to a cable running up to the massive steel boom that overhung the platform. On the command "Go!" he leaped off the platform and swung beneath the boom. On command, he carried out the correct procedure for "Collision to your front", "Collision to your left", "... your right", "... behind you", until the instructor was satisfied that the pupil would be able to avoid collisions with other parachutists in the air. Then the brake would be taken off and the cable would lower the pupil to the ground.

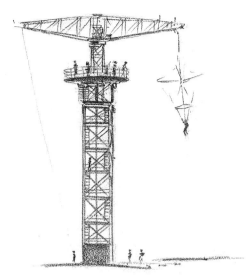

I mounted the innumerable steps to the platform and fastened the harness about me. My morale at this time was low. Just before starting the course I had ended a devastating love affair, the only-once-in-a-lifetime kind that leaves one drained at the time but is a source of remembered satisfaction in later life. However, at this time it was the end of the world for me and morale was at a low level on this particular day. I muttered to the instructor, "Make it a good loud 'Go'."

He looked back at me with one of those piercing, soul-stripping, level gazes that only a regular NCO can give. Then he said, "You don't need any extra help." A short pause, then, "Remember that there are more pebbles on the beach than were ever picked up. *GO!*"

As I swung in my harness I wondered how the devil did he know about it? I hadn't told a soul! But that was the very high calibre of the instructors at Abingdon: they handled a new course every two weeks, yet they seemed to know each of us individually as the strong and weak personalities that we were.

After the tower we moved over to the pulley. This consisted of a wooden platform twenty feet high erected on sloping ground. A steel cable ran past it above head-height, following the downward slope of the ground. The inevitable harness was attached to a pulley running on the wire. The pupil stood on the platform, donned the harness, and at the command "Go!" leaped off the platform at right angles to the wire. The pulley with pupil attached ran off down the slope. On the way the pupil was shaken to and fro "like a rat", as the instructor put it. This was to simulate the buffeting one occasionally experienced in the slipstream when jumping from an aeroplane. I rather enjoyed the sensation. Gay abandon is the best summing up of the pulley and wire.

The balloon was the next major obstacle. If there were to be any more refusals on the course they would come here. It was an old wartime barrage balloon with a canvas-covered gondola or, as it was officially called, a cage, with a canvas roof and an open door space at one end. Inside it were rails to clutch for support. Above the door space was a horizontal steel bar, one inch in diameter and about fifteen inches long, known as the "strong point". Attached to the strong point were six clips, one for the despatcher and one for each of the full load of five parachutists. The balloon was wound up and down on a steel cable by a petrol-driven winch. Normal jumping height was 800 feet, and on the way up, it lurched and tilted at a morale-lowering angle. The floor sloped towards the door space and gave the feeling that one could fall out.

When his turn came, each pupil stood on the door space as a solo performer. Five other people in the cage were all within touching distance, yet as he stood in the door, toecap projecting over the edge, one hand on the outside surface of the cage, balloon above, earth 800 feet below, the jumper was utterly alone, isolated within his own capability and will power. No-one would push or help him out. When the word "Go!" was barked in his ear, he alone had to make the instant decision and leap out.

Five trainees marched in single file towards the balloon cage resting on the ground beneath the enormous, tethered bulk of barrage balloon that

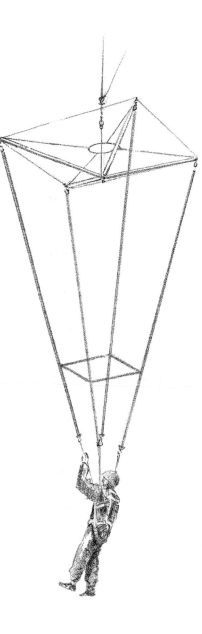

would soon lift it to 800 feet. With banter or in silence, according to his temperament, each man took his place in the cage. The static lines that would open the parachutes were pulled out a few feet from the parachute packs to enable the despatcher to clip them to the strong point above the open door space. When all five were secured the despatcher tugged at each one, "OK number one?" "Number one OK", "OK number two?" and so on until each man had seen his line tugged against the strong point and answered in the affirmative. Then the bar was secured across the door space. The bar was a piece of mild steel, an inch wide and a quarter of an inch thick, that fastened across the gaping door space at waist level. "Up eight hundred, five men jumping!" the despatcher called. "Up eight hundred, five men jumping!" replied the winch driver, and let in the clutch.

With a lurch that tilted the floor down towards the door, the cage rose from the ground. I was jumping number three. I gripped the handrail tightly and started to pray, silently, to myself, "Our Father who art in heaven . . .". I hate the way the floor slopes downwards towards the cage door when the balloon is rising . . .

"I want to see some good exits today," said the despatcher, "and when you go, look up and watch your canopy developing."

The balloon contined to rise steadily, inexorably. "Hallowed be thy name . . ." The floor was sloping now less steeply. Gradually, seen through the door, the landscape opened out. One could now see beyond the hedge bounding the far end of the dropping zone.

"Thy kingdom come . . .

The despatcher, after a last check downwards at the dropping zone safety officer who was slowly waving the yellow flag to and fro, grinned and began, "Did I ever tell you the story of the man who bought a puppy? No? Well there was this man . . ."

The fields had now opened out so that each succeeding field stretched out beyond the immediate landscape to the further distance where the field boundaries were not so sharply defined, and where the early morning sun glinted on distant farm roofs and hidden stretches of water.

"So the man decided to take the puppy to the vet . . ."

"Thy will be done, on earth . . ."

"So the vet says . . ."

". . . as it is in heaven . . ."

The balloon was now at 400 feet, and the wind was a little stronger than it had been at ground level. I began to relax my grip on the handrail. I looked at my companions, steel-helmeted, camouflaged-smocked, who were apparently enthralled by the joke the despatcher was telling. The canvas covering the cage was now flapping and rippling in the wind at 500 feet.

Somewhere between ". . . as it is in heaven . . ." and "lead us not into temptation . . .", between "So the vet says . . ." and the ludicrous ending of the joke, my tension began to relax. True, the heart that kept my body supplied with blood was pounding harder and faster than usual, but I myself, the person, felt a calmness, an all-enveloping confidence. My eyes locked onto those of the despatcher and there passed between us an understanding such as only occurs between men in the high places above the earth. The same sort of sympathy occurs in rock climbing, although the men may be out of sight of each other, separated by a rocky wall but joined

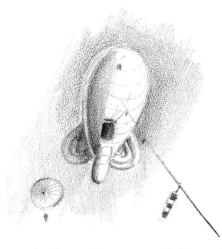

by the rope that has become to each of them an extension of his senses, a link in his communication with his fellow man.

The balloon was now at 600 feet. Tiny, foreshortened men moved about on the edge of the DZ. 800 feet. With a last lurch the balloon had arrived. Down on the DZ a small figure was now waving a blue flag slowly to and fro, in an arc around his body. This was the signal that it was all clear to start jumping.

The despatcher removed the steel pin securing the bar, which fell with a clatter against the left-hand edge of the door. "Number one! Stand in the door!" A brief pause, then, "Number one! Go!" The first soldier leaped out and vanished downwards. The static line thumped taut, then slackened, and with one jerk of his right hand the despatcher had it back inboard and stowed in the corner of the cage.

Number two was already walking gingerly towards the door. He positioned himself. "Go!" and he was gone. I moved into the door. I carefully positioned the toecap of my right boot projecting over the edge of the floor, looking down as I did so. My right hand was flat against the outside surface of the cage on the right side of the door. My left hand gripped the seam of my left trouser leg – this was the drill in those days before reserve parachutes. I looked up. Twenty feet away the heavy mooring ropes at the tail of the balloon hung down, swaying and twitching in the breeze. Beyond them in the vast distance the edge of the world dissolved in a grey-blue blur into

a pale, misty sky. For a tangible moment I was perfectly still, poised. Then I thrust myself outwards.

As my right hand flashed across my body to grip my left wrist, I looked up and saw for a fleeting instant the despatcher's face staring down at me. Then the moments of development imprinted themselves indelibly within me. I saw the white nylon rigging lines come shimmying down out of the pack now suspended on the end of the static line. Then came the slower undulation of the olive-green canopy as it pulled out, then suddenly burst wide open, partially crumpled up, and then re-inflated, stopping me with a firm tug so that my feet swung up. Then I was suspended beneath a great, solid dome of canopy, solid save for the eighteen-inch diameter apex vent through which I could see the blue of the sky.

In leisurely fashion I reached up to the front lift webs (it wouldn't do to be seen making a panic grab for them) and by pushing on one and pulling on the other was able to turn my body so that I could look behind me at the balloon cable. Satisfied that I was drifting clear of it, I settled down to assess the direction and speed of my horizontal drift.

I was travelling forwards but not fast. I shifted my hands onto the back lift webs and began to pull gently downwards. The horizontal drift stopped. I was coming vertically down. Easing up slightly, I allowed a small forward component to assist my landing roll. The ground moved upwards, faster, then faster. An oscillation developed. I damped it out with a strong pull on one lift web. Feet and knees together! Keep your elbows in! Feet turned at forty-five degrees to the line of flight! With a crash I landed (landings were not my forte). My parachute collapsed beside me. In the air were two more parachutists. Five more were lined up at the edge of the field, awaiting their turn. The balloon began to descend.

There were some who hated parachuting from a balloon. There were others who rather liked it. I belonged to the latter group, although I always approached the balloon with some fear. A descent from a balloon was, in every sense of the word, a solo performance. It was a chance to achieve perfection at every stage, at the exit, flight and landing. There was none of the noise, flap and rush of an exit from a military aeroplane with fourteen other parachutists behind me, fourteen brains with only one predominant throught overriding all else: "Out! Through that door! Out!" From the balloon cage there was all the time in the world to get a good position in the door, a comfortable position, an exactly poised position, without the moral and physical pressure of an aeroplane load of eager young paratroopers.

There were some who, when called forward to the door of the balloon cage, would step forward and a second later would be gone. And the good despatcher would sense the man's desire to get it over with quickly and would give the command "Go!" the instant he was poised in the door. There were others who liked to extract the maximum of sensation from the exit, who would position themselves precisely, exactly, and look down at the earth, then straight out in front, and finally would despatch themselves without the need for the imperative "Go!" to be barked six inches from their left ear. These were the parachutists as distinct from paratroopers. These were the ones to whom parachuting was much more than a means of conveying soldiers from point A up here to point B down there. This is not to say that we never experienced apprehension, or full-blown fear. We did! We just had our different ways of overcoming it.

We wore only one parachute in those days. There was no reserve parachute, only the well-tried X type parachute on our backs. We had been told that "they open with monotonous regularity", and we believed it. There was no problem with the parachute. We trusted it absolutely. The problem was deep inside ourselves. From the day we were born we have only one inborn, natural fear — the fear of falling. It is the only fear a baby has. All other fears are learned by experience. We were now being asked, nay ordered, to overcome this natural fear. We did so because of the very high standard of teaching and of the instructors at No. 1 Parachute School, RAF Abingdon.

Three jumps from the balloon were followed by five from a Hastings aeroplane. The Hastings was a four-engined transport aircraft carrying thirty men plus crew. There was a door exit on each side of the fuselage.

Over the door were fixed the red and green jumping lights, four seconds of red warning followed by the green executive command to jump. One leaped out as forcefully as possible straight into the powerful slipstream of the inboard engine on that side of the fuselage. Then, as one fell away behind and below the aeroplane, the static line opened the parachute and one dangled below the parachute canopy in a silence that was a welcome relief from the grinding roar of four piston engines.

On one of these five flights we were jumping "simultaneous sixes", that is six men jumping from the port door at the same time as six men leaped out from the starboard door. I was in the second six so I was able to watch the stick ahead of me. The last man on the starboard side walked manfully to the open door space and then made a half-hearted attempt at an exit. He was halfway through the door when he changed his mind and tried to get back in again. He stood there, half in and half out of the aircraft, pinned against the rear edge of the door by the force of the slipstream from the starboard inner propeller. Then suddenly he vanished through the door and we heard above the racket of the engine noise "bump, scrape, bump, thud" along the outside of the fuselage. It was so funny I laughed out aloud. The despatcher caught my eye and shouted, "It's called 'beating retreat'!" I was still chuckling as I made my own way to the door during the next circuit of the aeroplane over the dropping zone. Arriving at the door, I looked down at the ground a thousand feet below. Suddenly I wasn't laughing any more.

I cannot remember very much about my own first exit from a Hastings. I know that there was an absolute certainty in my mind that I would jump. Then as I leaped into the slipstream there was a feeling of enormous, irresistible, all-engulfing power, as the turbulent, roaring, air snatched at me and thrust and carried me away behind the aircraft. These are the only two things I can remember about that first aircraft jump.

Afterwards, safe on the ground, I experienced a feeling of exhilaration. It was more than that. It was a compound of exhilaration, happiness, buoyancy. It was a joy so intense that it physically hurt inside my chest. It was exciting, thrilling, ecstatic. It satisfied. It gratified. It was mental, physical and spiritual all combined in one sensation. I had never experienced a feeling so intense before. I haven't since. It lasted for about an hour, gradually diminishing in intensity. So deeply is it recorded in my memory that I can recall it in detail whenever I want to and relish it again and again, and I find that my pulse is pounding and my breathing quick and difficult.

All parachutists experience this exhilaration to some degree. As one becomes a more experienced parachutist the intensity of feeling is less and it lasts for a shorter time, but it is still there after every jump.

With these eight jumps, three from the balloon and five from the aeroplane, we had completed the course. It had been interesting, exciting, frightening, mentally and physically hard work, and in retrospect very enjoyable. The eight jumps entitled us to wear the much-coveted parachute wings, insignia of the qualified military parachutist. Of course, there was very much more to learn about tactical military jumping, but at least one was recognised as a "parachutist", entitled to extra parachute pay. One was now "para", "qualified", "one of us".

We sewed our wings onto our right sleeves in double quick time, and returned home in high spirits. We had done it! We were the best, the most, the greatest! Morale was high. We had a floating feeling. We had that self-confidence that comes of being of the best that there is.

3

WINGS OF PRIDE

I was now a parachutist, a very new and immature parachutist, but none the less a parachutist. I had now earned the right to wear the cap badge and wings insignia of the Parachute Regiment. So I reported back again to my TA unit in high spirits, unaware of how little I really knew about parachuting, and particularly about military parachuting. In the next few years in the TA, I was to learn.

Our pride in our regiment was high and it was soon acquired by men who like myself had previously served with other regiments. I remember once hearing the RSM arguing with the battalion second-in-command. They were discussing the concept of the parent regiment. "But Mr Lawrence," said the 2 i/c, "all of us start off in some other regiment and that is our parent regiment. Some of us are ex-South Lancs, some are ex-King's Regiment. Those are our parent regiments. You can't say that this is your parent regiment."

"Sir," said RSM Lawrence, throwing out his not inconsiderable chest, "I am a parachutist!" We, who overheard, secretly applauded.

That perhaps was the key to our regimental pride. We were all parachutists, entitled to wear parachute wings on our uniform sleeves, the badge of the qualified military parachutist. It gave an added spring to our step. We walked taller. We considered ourselves better than other men, non-parachutists. And, in fact, we were.

In the Parachute Regiment, regular and territorial, the common bond between all ranks was that we all, without exception, had made premeditated jumps from aeroplanes in flight. Sweat, fear and a thousand feet of fresh air beneath one's boots are great levellers of rank. And if that isn't enough, the average Merseyside parachutist's sense of humour will soon pull the mat out from under anyone who gets a bit uppity. That is not to say that the soldiers had no respect for their officers and NCOs. On the contrary, they had, and they would be positively protective towards a young second lieutenant who was finding the going a bit rough.

From time to time young officers would apply for a transfer from their own units into our battalion of the Parachute Regiment. Before they could be accepted by us they had to prove they were physically and mentally fit enough. These qualities were assessed by means of tests carried out over a very strenuous weekend at a Weekend Training Centre; with its love of abbreviations the Army called these establishments WETCs.

One set of tests was known as the confidence tests. These were simple and straightforward tests of confidence in oneself, for example, a leap from one platform to another one nearby, but high up in the air, maybe fifty feet above the ground, swinging from one high perch to another via a rope thrown across by the previous man. Each test was demonstrated twice by an instructor, and then the recruits had to do it.

One evening after training I went up to the Mess. The CO, Lt Col Pat O'Kane, was there looking worried. Although I was only a junior officer I asked him what was up.

He told me, "I'm worried about a young subaltern who wants to transfer to us from another regiment. He's everything a young English officer should be. He's fit, well trained, carries himself well, plays cricket for his county and all that sort of thing. But he hesitated on the confidence tests at the weekend just gone by. He did everything else perfectly. He just wasn't happy on the confidence tests. I just don't know what to do, Peter."

"You must reject him, Sir," I replied without hesitation.

"Why do you say that?"

"Well Sir, if you accept him he will some day be in command of a stick of troops in an aircraft. If he hesitates then with fourteen other men behind him, he could delay their exits long enough for the last few men to overshoot the DZ and maybe land in power lines or on a railway line or in a river. They could be killed or injured. You must reject him."

He thought for a moment, then he said, "You're quite right," and the subject was closed.

Pat O'Kane was later killed in a parachuting accident. He was by then commanding the regular brigade. Just before he left to take up another appointment he decided to make a farewell jump with the brigade in an exercise. He didn't have to jump. It was just his fine nature to make such a gesture.

Although in our training as parachute soldiers we were sometimes cold, wet, hungry, sleepless and thoroughly fed up, there were moments of impressive spectacle, even beauty, that more than made up for the discomforts of military training.

I remember one fine evening during an annual camp in the vast training area in Norfolk, watching one of the other brigades start a two-day exercise. It was half an hour before sunset on a fine July evening. The sky to the east was pale, clear and empty. Then the first three aircraft arrived, flying in a vee formation about a mile away from us. They flew steadily in formation over the dropping zone, dropping tiny objects that blossomed into parachutes. In half a minute there were ninety men in the air. As the first three aeroplanes cleared the DZ another three started their dropping run. Soon there were four layers of men in the air. And as the first layer was landing, a fifth layer spilled out into the evening sky: three hundred and sixty men in the air at a time and more continually arriving, an instant army where two minutes before there had been only empty sky. The setting sun reflected off their parachute canopies and sparkled off the polished aluminium of the aeroplanes. Then there was silence. The last aeroplane had gone. The last of the troops were landing. Ten minutes later they had vanished into the darkening shadows of the evening, leaving their discarded parachutes lying on the ground as the only evidence that a few minutes previously more than two thousand men had passed this way.

Although we were used to this sort of thing, we had stood watching, mostly silent, spellbound by the transient beauty of the spectacle.

4

ON EXERCISE

Although there was an intrinsic beauty in what we saw on that July evening in Norfolk, it was no joy ride and fun jump for the soldiers taking part. This was military parachuting, the aim being to drop hundreds, even thousands, of soldiers in the right place at the right time, with all their weapons, equipment and communications in good working order. Before the drop there would have been weeks of planning and preparations. At the take-off airfield there would have been hours of waiting. Time to think, time to catch up on sleep lying on the grass with one's head resting on a parachute, time perhaps to see in one's surroundings traces and relics of a nostalgic, bygone era.

On one exercise we were to take off from an old, abandoned, wartime airfield. It consisted of a concrete control tower, some Nissen huts, a few small brick buildings, some underground air-raid shelters and three concrete runways. There were still a few hours to go before take-off and I used them to explore the airfield.

First I made for the control tower. There was a steel staircase, black and rusty, on the outside of the grey building. It was blocked with a tangle of green creeper that grew from cracks in the concrete, from the walls and from underneath the steps. A broken door swung to and fro in the gentle breeze. Inside it was emptiness. The windows, opaque with dirt, were cracked and ugly with missing glass. I forced my way up the iron steps to a little landing and stood there awhile, my camouflage-patterned smock, olive-green trousers and red beret seeming out of place on this airfield that had once throbbed with aircraft noise and with the shouts and laughter of young men and women dressed in the blue uniform of the RAF and WAAF.

I looked out over the runways, cracked and speckled with tiny yellow flowers of a rock plant that seemed to thrive on bare concrete and desolation. And as the afternoon drew towards evening, the breeze faded and a warm, sunlit stillness held the whole airfield in a timeless moment in which I seemed to sense the ghosts of an earlier time going about their duties, refuelling and re-arming aircraft, giving quiet instructions over the wireless from the tower, orderlies cycling between office and stores, and an occasional truck driving along the perimeter track.

A deserted airfield is a sad place. Once it had a life of its own when men and women worked together for the common purpose of defeating the enemy. Now it is gaunt, stilled, barren. A place of memory or of imagination, a decayed place. Then the breeze stirred again and the mood passed.

I returned to the kitting-up area, a stretch of perimeter track on which the parachutes had been laid out earlier. I recognised my own kit at the end of one of the lines. My X-type parachute pack was lying on its neatly folded harness. On top of the X-type was my reserve parachute and on top of that my steel helmet containing my brown leather gloves. They had two purposes. Firstly I wore them to avoid any friction burns that might result from a bad exit from the aeroplane, and secondly they would keep my hands warm during the long, hard nights ahead. Alongside the parachutes lay the dark green terylene weapons container that held my personal kit, weapon, ammunition and food for the next two days.

All around me troops were fitting their parachutes, taking in leg-straps,

31

letting out waist-straps, pulling down lock-buckles on shoulder-straps, checking nylon ties and adjusting their helmet chin-straps. The last rays of the afternoon sun slanted across the men, picking out lined features in otherwise youthful faces. On the runway it glinted on the metal of the aeroplanes, sculpting their form with light and shadow and mirror-like highlights. The sky was clear apart from some high-flying wisps of cirrus and a faint yellowish haze in the west. We marched out to our respective aircraft, our movements heavy with the loads we carried.

One has plenty of time at this stage to reflect. There is time to run over the briefing again and to remind oneself of the things to be checked to ensure a safe descent to earth. There is also ample time in which to feel afraid. Fear

and parachuting are inseparable: as the Padre once remarked, "Parachuting is thirty minutes of mounting misery followed by thirty seconds of pure joy."

One knows of course that the parachute will open. It always has done in the past. It always will do in the future. Of course it will! And anyway it can't happen to me. If there's going to be an accident it will happen to someone else. I shan't die one micro-second before my time. In any case my reactions are extremely fast. (Stop rationalising! You're scared and there's nothing you can do about it. So get on with it! The other stick's already emplaning.)

I turned to my stick of troops and barked, "Port stick! Left turn! Lead on." (It would have to be the port side of the aircraft. I hate port exits.) We walked towards the Hastings, our weapons containers, great ungainly bundles weighing anything up to ninety or more pounds, hoisted up onto our shoulders.

I boarded the 'plane last and took my seat just forward of the door on the port side of the fuselage. The troops sat on folding, metal bench seats that lined the sides of the fuselage from the cabin bulkhead down to the doors. I fastened my seat belt, and watched my troops. I wondered if they, too, felt as I did, uneasy, apprehensive, dry-mouthed. They seemed cheerful enough.

Then the despatchers came bustling down the fuselage, handing to each man a strop. The strop consisted of thick webbing an inch and a half wide and twenty feet long with a hook at its end. Its purpose was to extend the normal static line of the X-type parachute so that the parachutist was well clear of the tail of the aircraft before the parachute began to leave its pack. Each parachutist would later clip the D-ring at the end of his static line into the hook and position the safety pin that would prevent the hook accidentally opening.

The aircrew came aboard and stalked up the fuselage to the cabin. Then I listened to the noises of the four-engined aeroplane being started up. One by one the engines fired, and by twisting my neck I could just see the port outer propeller through the small circular porthole over my left shoulder. The boarding ladder was pulled up and stowed. The doors were closed and the air quartermaster spoke into his intercom. The aeroplane moved with a gentle bumping around the perimeter track to the end of the runway. The engines revved up, then throttled down. Then they opened up again and the aeroplane moved forward, gathering speed. The acceleration pushed us sideways towards the tail of the aircraft. The airfield fence passed below, then a road and houses. We were safely airborne.

There was exactly one hour to go before P-hour, the time at which we would have to jump from the security of the aeroplane into the tearing slipstream of the inner propellers at an airspeed of about 120 knots. There were sixty minutes in which to think about it.

I let my eyes roam down the opposite side of the fuselage, eyeing each soldier in turn. Some were already asleep – a protective device. Some were chatting, leaning towards each other and speaking the words into their

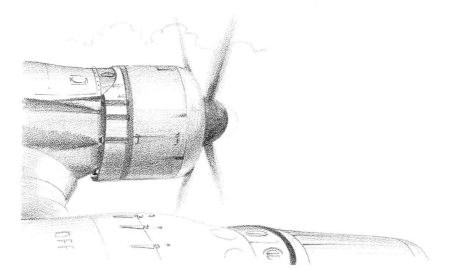

neighbours' ears above the noise of the engines. Some were looking out of the ports, their bodies twisted round, seat-belts now unfastened, pointing out features of the landscape to each other. Others, a few, were fidgeting. When their eyes met mine they forced a smile, and I knew, and smiled back at them. But by and large they appeared to be a tough, cheerful lot and I was proud to be one of them. We were all volunteers, thirty or so men, each weighted down with a hundredweight or more of equipment including weapons container, main parachute and the new-fangled reserve parachute.

I found myself yawning. I always yawned when I felt apprehensive. Every man in the Parachute Regiment would agree that he was afraid before a parachute jump. There was, in fact, a saying in the Regiment: "A man who says he isn't afraid before a parachute jump is either a fool or a liar." Each man had his fears, from the general down to the most junior private soldier. Each had his own way of dealing with his fear. Some slept. Others conversed. A few just stared ahead and from time to time swallowed.

Others, like me, rationalised their fears. I told myself that fear was just the output signal of the brain's warning system. My brain, in effect, was saying to me that what I was about to do carried certain inherent risks, that the brain wasn't pleased with the body that housed it and transported it around, taking the sort of physical chances of which the brain disapproved.

This warning signal took the form, in my case, of a tightening of the diaphragm and a bitter taste at the back of the mouth. I swallowed more than usual, and I yawned. Then I would become critical of the pilot's handling of the aeroplane. I would regard the despatchers as a fussy lot who bustled up and down, checking this and that, and I would be glad to jump out of this aeroplane and leave its damn-fool pilot and his brood of clucking, fussing despatchers hanging at the stall point while I took to the safety of my parachute.

Then I would check for the umpteenth time that my harness quick-release box was really locked, and tell myself to stop being a fool and leave the damned thing alone. And anyway, I couldn't allow myself to show fear because I carried three pips on my shoulders. So I rationalised and swallowed and yawned and nodded and smiled at the troops. At the back of my mind I knew that whatever happened, I would jump through that door. When the time came, I knew that I, the person, could always over-ride my brain and its warnings and forebodings. So I settled down and dozed.

I awoke to the sound of rushing air and looking up, saw that the doors on both sides of the fuselage had been removed and now lay on the floor at the tail end of the aeroplane. I wiped the taste of sleep from my mouth and waited, feeling tense. Then the air quartermaster with both arms gestured "Stand up", and I just caught the shouted command, "Prepare for action!"

As I stood up my fears abated, as they always did and as I knew they always would. I clipped my weapons container into the quick-release hooks on my harness and circled the leg-strap tightly about my lower thigh. I checked that the static line from the top of my parachute ran clear of snags to the strop, and that the safety pin that held it was firmly fixed. Then I passed it back to the man behind me, who passed his strop to the man behind him, and so on down the stick. I heard the order, "Tell off for equipment check", and waited for it to come up the stick and for the man behind me to tap my right shoulder and shout, "Two OK!" Then I raised my right hand and shouted, "One OK, port stick OK!"

The air quartermaster ordered, "Action stations", and both sticks moved forward in that peculiar shuffling step known in those days as "the Abingdon samba", until the two stick commanders were standing a pace away from the open door space on our respective sides of the aeroplane.

By now the fear had gone. Once the time for action arrived, the brain, realising the futility of any further warnings, resigned itself to the fact that its owner was about to hurl himself out of an aeroplane, and it ceased its efforts to remind me of my folly. Recognising what had happened, I smiled slightly and gave myself to the enjoyment of the moment.

I stood at the head of fourteen other soldiers, all ready to follow me out of the door. I stood with left foot slightly in advance of my right foot, left hand holding the top of the door space, right hand gripping the handle of my

weapons container, and waited. The Hastings winged on at an altitude of 1200 feet. Looking out from the door space, I tried to pick up landmarks.

I tried to visualise the map I had studied in the briefing room. The run in was to be west-to-east. That meant that with a normal exit and canopy development I was likely to be facing west when my parachute developed. P-hour was 1930, so the early-evening sun would be in the west. Then with the sun in front of me, the straight white road should be on my right and the rectangular wood on my left. Funny how the colours of the land seemed to be intensified when one stood at the door. It was like the exaggeration of colour in a projected colour transparency. The aircraft now seemed to be remarkably steady. There, just coming into view under the trailing edge of the wing – a white road. That must be it.

I drew back a little from the door so that I could see the red and green jumping lights at the top of the door jamb. I was now a single-purpose machine awaiting a light signal. The aeroplane was very steady now. It was quieter, too, all of a sudden. The red light glowed strongly. For four seconds it glowed, then it went out and the green came on. I leaped through the door.

The slipstream gripped me and turned me through ninety degrees so that I faced aft, and hurled me back along the aeroplane's track. I saw the under-surface of the tailplane, dark grey, pass overhead. There was a firm tugging at my shoulders, my legs came up before my face, I saw the flash of white canopy billow out and inflate. I felt once again that savage satisfaction that accompanies the canopy's development. I reached up and grasped the front lift webs and pushed and pulled to turn from one side to the other, searching the air around me for other parachutists. Seeing that I was clear, I released my weapons container, which dropped to the end of its nylon rope and swung beneath me. Then I settled down to assess my drift over the ground, searched for obstacles and got ready for landing. I found time in all this activity to get my bearings from the road, the wood and the position of the sun. Then I hit the ground and rolled. I lay on the ground, released my harness and, still in the prone position, quickly removed my rifle from the weapons container and fitted my equipment. Then substituting a red beret for my steel helmet, I loped off the DZ towards my RV at the western end of the rectangular wood.

5

A NIGHT DROP

During my TA service I made one hundred parachute jumps. Most of them were made in daylight, but a few were at night.

There is a magic in being above the earth at night. As one relaxes in a window seat in the luxury of a jet aircraft, all within is light and warmth. Outside, the dark earth is speckled with lights – white tungsten or orange sodium lights in clusters, an isolated gleam marking the lonely farmhouse – while looking upwards, the airborne traveller may see the twinkling points of light by which in more leisurely days the pilot of his aeroplane might have navigated.

On this particular night I was not travelling in the smoothness of jet flight high above the earth. We were attending annual camp and were to make a night parachute descent as part of our parachute continuation training. So I was seated on the hard, cold, metal, folding bench seat of a Royal Air Force Transport Command Hastings aircraft, winging through the night air above a desolate, featureless moorland at two o'clock in the morning. At this dark hour one's spirits are said to be at their lowest ebb. This is the hour of blackness and despair at which for some unfortunate wretch the prospect of facing another day becomes an impossibility. But my spirits at that hour were high. I was completely absorbed in the sights, sounds and activities around me.

The aeroplane would make five runs over the dropping zone, dropping six parachutists on each run. The start of the dropping run would be marked on the DZ by paraffin flares set in the pattern of a "T". The end of the DZ would be marked by a short line of flares, a bar. The drop would be clean fatigue, i.e. with no military equipment, and I would lead the last stick of six men.

In the dim interior lighting from small circular lamps set in the ceiling of the fuselage I watched the first stick getting ready to jump. They stood up, six bulky, steel-helmeted figures, clad in camouflage smocks and green denim trousers. At the rear end of the aircraft the RAF air quartermaster was speaking into his intercom. Then he straightened up, clipped a broad webbing safety belt about his middle and removed the port door. The night sky showed, grey, faintly luminescent, in the upright space where the door had been, and the night air rushed past.

The despatcher shouted "Action stations!" and six men moved down to the door. Number one took up his position at the door, his hands upstretched, grasping the top of the door frame. The lights went out. In absolute blackness save for the faint greyness of the night sky visible through the door, the Hastings roared on through the darkness. It was as though all life had ceased except for this cocoon of noise and vibration that carried thirty men and its crew above the darkened earth. Six men standing up, facing aft. The remainder seated, watching them.

The engines' roar softened. A tension built up in the darkened cabin. Then suddenly the entire interior was flooded with dim red light as the red warning lights flashed on. For four seconds everything, every man, was frozen in a red tableau. Then the red went out and was replaced by an eerie green glow from the jumping lights. Six dim green figures moved purposefully through the door aperture. Six young men bathed in green light leaped strongly into the night, and the door space was empty.

The engine note hardened and the white cabin lighting came on again. The aeroplane turned onto a wide circuit that would take perhaps five minutes to bring it once more over the dropping zone. Three more times the 'plane spawned into the night sky, and then it was our turn.

We six parachutists stood up and went through the ritual of checks, orders and replies that is an essential preliminary to military parachuting. Then we moved along to the door space and the lights went out again.

Up to this moment I had been very much aware that I was a part of a group, that there was a strong bond of comradeship binding together these men who sat and stood so close to each other in the confines of the aeroplane. But now as I stood at their head, my hands resting lightly at the top of the door frame, my left foot slightly forward, I was no longer aware of their presence. I was alone in a wonderful metal flying machine from which I would presently spring into the darkness outside. As I stood there, the night wrapped itself around me. From time to time little eddies of night air whispered round the edge of the door. Below was absolute blackness. Above was the faint luminosity of the overcast night sky. The aeroplane droned on and the night became a tangible thing that neither frightened nor encouraged but had some magical quality that breathed a sense of peace. The night is neutral. It is what happens in our brains that makes the night whatever it is to each of us. To me the night was tranquillity. And so I stood, immobile, waiting for the order that would enable me to embrace the night in one forceful leap.

My ears, attuned for a change of sound from the motors, alerted my brain. A sudden tensing of the nerves warned that at any moment now the signal would be given. I looked up at the pair of lamp glasses above the door, one red and one green.

The red glowed on. I stepped right into the door, tense. Without seeing it I knew the instant that the red glow changed to green, and I was out, forcing my way through the slipstream into the dark torrent of air battering back from the propellers. Then a strong, firm pull at my shoulders, and silence assured me that my parachute had developed. This was the silence of an absolute absence of sound. Somewhere above was cloud base. Somewhere below was the earth. Strung out in a line behind me, invisible in the night, were five other men.

Twisting around in my harness, I saw the flares marking the DZ. Nearby, a "T". In the distance, a horizontal bar that marked the far end of the DZ. Tiny, yellow, flickering lights set in a background of black. The other parachutists were still invisible. I settled myself to concentrate on the descent and landing. There were no visual references of any sort except for the yellow flames of the paraffin flares. I estimated my drift from the apparent movement of the flares, but had no idea of my height. The flares swayed to

and fro. I concentrated hard on looking at them. They now remained fixed and I realised that it was myself that was swinging from side to side with the oscillation of the canopy. I pulled on the lift webs to damp out the oscillation and set my feet for the landing. The flares were now noticeably moving upwards towards me. The last fifty feet vanished in a rush. There was a confused jumble of sensations – impact, a flare seemingly overhead, grass in my face, cold damp dew, the nylon canopy across my legs, the thud of another parachutist landing nearby.

I stood up. There were distant voices, torch beams, the sound of a three-ton lorry in low gear. I folded my parachute and slung it over my shoulder. Then I walked slowly towards the edge of the field, breathing deeply of the cold, pre-dawn air.

Again it was a night-time exercise. The soft Mediterranean night air flowed gently over the beautiful island of Cyprus. We were to jump soon after dawn. In a grass area lit by the yellow glare of sodium lamps rigged for the occasion, we fitted our parachutes, lined up in our previously designated sticks. On my left was a major from another unit who would be jumping number one. On my right was a corporal and the remainder of the stick. I began to check my parachute.

First of all I examined the three nylon ties holding the pack shut. The one in the centre held the flaps together where the static line entered the pack. The other two ties were at the top corners where the lift webs emerge. These three ties had to be intact. Next I inspected the harness. No broken or cracked buckles, no fraying, the stitching looked good, and the quick-release box worked. I had just started to adjust the harness to my own fit when there was a cry for help from the major, who was in what an onlooker later described as "a hell of a state". I disentangled him from his harness, showed him what was wrong, and returned to the adjustment of my own harness.

The first thing to do when adjusting the harness of the X-type parachute is to slide the two shoulder-buckles up or down on the webbing until they rest on the corners of the stiff backing of the parachute pack. This ensures that the parachutist is suspended from the top of his shoulders in an upright position. If the buckles are adjusted too far back, the parachutist descends in a leaning-forward position. If they are too far forwards, being suspended from in front of his shoulders, he will descend in a slightly back-lying position.

The next thing to adjust is the waist-belt and finally the leg-straps. Lengthening the waist-belt and shortening the leg-straps has the effect of lowering the quick-release box in which the two halves of the waist-belt and the leg-straps meet and are secured by lugs. The best position for the box is at the waist. Down there it feels comfortable and does not press upon the diaphragm or restrict the breathing. So I moved the buckles of the leg-straps right up to the seat-strap.

The gallant major again called for help. I left my parachute and went to assist. I didn't really mind the major's flap. It took my mind off things. An RAF parachuting instructor arrived, pulled a face and helped the major out of his parachute. Having trussed up the major to his own satisfaction, the RAF sergeant checked me. He tested the tightness and fit of my harness, grunted and passed on to number three. I let out my breath, unflexed my muscles, removed my red beret from inside my smock where it had been padding under the quick-release box, and contracted to my normal size again. The harness now felt comfortable.

We completed our preparations and marched out into the darkness beyond the sodium floodlights towards the silent, brooding aeroplanes. The time was now 0430 with still an hour to go before take-off. We put down our containers, removed our parachutes and laid them down in two rows. Then we strolled onto the grass to gossip and perhaps to turn a back and attend to a call of nature. I walked off a little into the darkness and sniffed at the night air, calm, warm, balmy, with a faint pleasant scent of the Cyprus countryside. I could hear the murmur of voices, an occasional laugh. A few hundred yards away, figures moved in the pool of orange light around the kitting-up area. I strolled back and forth, breathing deeply.

Soon the dark sky lightened into grey and I could see the troops clustered about the aeroplanes.

At 0520 we emplaned. At 0530 we took off into a bluish-grey sky, dark on one side, striped with pink and yellow on the other. Through the open door I could see the Mediterranean, flat, grey. Minutes later we passed over the Troodos Mountains, rugged, harsh, pink in the rising of the sun.

The old familiar aircraft drills began in preparation for the orderly exit of thirty soldiers from the aeroplane. There was more panic from the major. The leg-pin of his weapons container was jammed. Much advice, tugging and scraping with a knife solved this latest problem.

The Hastings was now flying due west, judging by the shadows cast by the sun. We stood up and moved down to the doors, the major number one of the starboard stick, myself number two and the rest of the stick pressed up close behind. Standing perhaps four feet away from the edge of the door, I could see the sandy coastline, the white creaming froth and then beyond it the blue of the sea merging gradually into grey at the horizon. Behind the beach were sand dunes, and inland of them was bright green grassland. The aeroplane's flaps were down and it seemed to have become very steady.

The despatcher gestured at the major to watch for the red and green lights. His eyes flickered between the dull lenses of the lights and the major's face. He glanced occasionally at the rest of the stick. The aircraft was now a little lower. The coast was nearer, too. We waited under the dragging burden of our weapons containers. The flaps were still down. Surely the aeroplane must be near the stall? Any moment now those lights must come on. The tip of the wing, glimpsed over the major's left shoulder, was so steady. The major dropped his gaze to the earth and then back to those still lifeless lights. I gripped one of the straps of my weapons container, warm, sweaty.

"Red on!" Four seconds of the red light. I felt the rest of the stick press up behind me bumper to bumper, military sardines before a green light opens the tin. Green flashed on, the major leaped out and swept away round the edge of the door. I stepped into the door, lunged through it and out.

In the instant of leaving the aircraft I knew I had made a bad exit. The slipstream shook me roughly. My canopy developed with a thump. I threw back my head just in time. As I did so, the lift webs from opposite shoulders crossed in front of my face. Looking up, I saw that the rigging lines were twisted into a solid rope for almost halfway up to the canopy. I began to kick my legs in an anti-clockwise direction to start my body spinning out of the twists. At the same time I pulled hard on the lift webs to separate them. With a jerk the rigging lines flew apart and the spinning stopped abruptly.

Then I became aware of a hideous pain that stabbed upwards into my guts and onwards up to my chest, making me feel sick. The buckles on my leg straps had clamped firmly onto my testicles, held there by my own weight. I shouted the one word, "God!" But on this occasion God was otherwise engaged. I pulled the leg-pin of my container, released the hooks and let it fall the length of the rope. The jerk at the end of the container's fall

shot another spasm of pain boring up through my body. The ground was close and it looked reasonable. No time or inclination for finesse. I thudded in a heap onto the grass. For several minutes I lay there, sweating and breathing hard. I sat up feeling both sick and furious.

The major walked by, jauntily. "I really enjoyed that," he said. "Had a marvellous exit and landing."

6

"A BIT HAIRY"

The situation was tricky. If I didn't talk my way out of it in the next thirty seconds I would be dead. There was no physical action that I could take to escape. All I could do as I swung in my parachute harness was talk clearly and convincingly to the soldier who was preparing to kill me. If I failed to convince him, or if he panicked, I would die.

The setting for this little drama was one of almost Wagnerian splendour. In the west, rays of late-afternoon sunshine slanted down through gaps in the storm clouds, spotlighting the landscape in yellows and greens and rimming the clouds with gold. To the east, against towering cloud ramparts, lightning flashed and thunder rumbled. Brilliant jagged fingers of forked lightning streaked and flickered across and through the clouds, while the thunderclaps cracked, rumbled and echoed in the vast valleys and caverns of the dark grey cloudscape. Overhead, forming an almost continuous background of noise, there was the roar of the powerful engines of the transport aeroplanes dropping their twin streams of steel-helmeted parachutists.

This training jump had started normally enough from a four-engined Hastings of RAF Transport Command. I had been number ten in the starboard stick, somewhere near the middle of the cargo of paratroops. I had shuffled down the fuselage on the command of the green jumping lights, had thrown aside the strop attached to number nine's static line as he turned into the door space, had placed a steadying hand on the outside of the cold metal skin of the aircraft and then hurled myself and my weapons container into the vibrant, rushing turbulence of the slipstream from the inboard propeller on the starboard side of the aeroplane.

My parachute had developed normally, its olive-green canopy firmly inflated. I had done all the right things in the right sequence. I had looked up and watched my canopy develop. All correct. Then I had reached up and grasped the front lift webs and pushed and pulled alternately to enable me to twist around and make all-round observation to ensure that I was clear of other parachutists.

Then to be absolutely safe, I had pulled hard on one set of lift webs so as to spill air out of one side of the canopy and thus drive it in the opposite direction to steer myself out of the stick altogether. I had then lowered my weapons container so that it dangled fifteen or twenty feet below me on its nylon rope and had settled down to judge my drift on the wind and prepare for the landing.

I watched the drift of the ground past the toecaps of my boots. I was drifting slowly forwards. Good! I would hold this position. The ground ahead at the estimated touch-down point was clear. The air was calm, the descent steady. Suddenly, for no reason at all, I looked upwards and backwards. Sliding across the sky towards me was another parachute, thirty feet or so higher than my own. Before I could do anything to escape, the other parachutist's weapons container crashed into the edge of my canopy. Then, as the other parachute slid directly above me into the downwards wake of my own 'chute, the container abruptly descended on its nylon rope and swung inside the cone of my rigging lines. The grey-green terylene bundle of equipment swung to and fro, bouncing from line to line. Then it swung outside and back again, its supporting rope now woven between the rigging lines. We two parachutists were inextricably joined.

I could see the shadowy form of the other parachutist through the fine woven nylon of my canopy. Then occasionally the other fellow would drift sideways and I was able to identify him as a member of my own platoon. Really! This was taking democracy too far.

The voice from above shouted, "Shall I jettison my weapons container?"

"No!" I yelled. "Hang on to it."

Feeling suddenly cold, I carefully examined the situation. The container dangling from the upper parachutist's harness was so tangled with the top end of my rigging lines that it was to all intents and purposes tied to them. If the upper parachutist jettisoned his container, my own canopy would instantly collapse upon me. The container, weighing about seventy-five pounds, would plummet to earth, followed by a streamer of fluttering nylon and rigging lines in which I would be enmeshed.

I watched the dark, greenish-grey bundle as it lashed to and fro inside my lines, and felt each impact down through the lift webs into my harness. The important thing was to stop the other fellow dropping his weapons container. I had to convince him that the best thing was to hang on to it. "We seem to be tied together," I said conversationally, "but we'll soon be down."

"Yes," he replied doubtfully. Then "I won't be able to land if I don't jettison it," he called to me.

"Yes you will. You can land on me! Just hold a good parachuting position until we land."

Silence for a few seconds, then "I think I'd better jettison it."

"No! You must hang on to it," I told him. "If you jettison, it will collapse my canopy. Hold on. We're nearly down."

I looked hard at the container lashing to and fro. It now had a distinct aspect of evil. That bundle of equipment, weapon and personal possessions could kill me. I think it was Dr Johnson who said that the contemplation of one's approaching death concentrates the mind wonderfully. He was absolutely right!

The ground was now much closer, about three hundred feet below, say ten to fifteen seconds away. I decided that at fifty feet I would jettison my own container which now swung on its rope below both of us. This would reduce the speed of our combined descent and would be a small complication out of the way.

Meanwhile I must prevent the other fellow from pulling the short webbing strap that would release his container rope from the leg-strap of his harness and allow it to drop. Another close look at the grey-green container confirmed it was securely snagged in my rigging lines. A quick glance around told me that we were away from other parachutists and that the landing area was reasonably clear. I looked up again at my companion who from time to time drifted sideways so that he was able to peer down at me over the edge of my canopy. "We're almost there," I said as casually as I could. "Only a few more seconds to go."

"What are you going to do?" he asked.

"I'm going to make a good landing and hope that you don't land on top of me."

"You'll be bloody lucky!"

"Yes. Now get your feet and knees together! Chin on chest! Elbows in! Hold a good parachuting position!"

The container continued to lash around inside my parachute, deforming the circular shape of the canopy. The other parachutist was silent but I could see that he was now holding a good parachuting position. The last hundred feet of the descent began to accelerate towards us – an optical illusion really, but it always seems as if the last few feet of height can't wait to vanish beneath a parachutist's feet.

"I'm going to jettison my container to give us a slower landing," I said. "You hang on to yours. Do you understand?"

"Yes."

At fifty feet I pulled the jettison release and watched my container fall away, thud on the ground and bounce.

"Now hold your parachuting position," I shouted, "and don't let go."

"It's OK," called the voice from above, "we'll be all right now."

We landed in a tangle of bodies, weapons container, canopies and rigging lines.

"Are you all right?" I asked him.

"Yes. Eh, that was a bit hairy, wasn't it, Sir?"

"It certainly was."

I lay for a minute or so on the ground, breathing hard, my heartbeat pounding. Then I slowly folded my canopy, plaited the rigging lines and stowed it roughly in the back-pack. Burdened with parachutes and weapons containers, we walked the half-mile to the track leading to the road where transport awaited us to take us back to barracks.

A jeep, empty but for the Training Major, bucked across the grass towards us as if to give us a lift. "Hurry up, Peter, the exercise will do you good," shouted the gallant major, accelerating away.

"Bloody swine," I snarled, but all my feelings were of elation at the new gift of life.

7

FALLING FREE

For some time there had been growing in me a strong desire to prolong the two or three seconds of fall before the static line-operated military parachute was fully open. I liked making my exit from the aircraft. It was such a forceful, exciting and absolutely irrevocable act. There was a tremendous sense of irresistible force in the slipstream pouring, battering, streaming back from the propellers. One had to force one's way out of the aeroplane into this tearing rush of air. (Dear God! The old excitement's there, just writing about it! I can hear again the rush and hiss of the air, feel the fluttering of loose folds of clothing, and see once more the glove ripped off my hand and hurled away by the 130-knot hurricane sweeping me down past the smooth, metal-skinned side of the aeroplane.)

The exception was of course jumping from the boom of the Blackburn Beverley. What a fantastic aeroplane that was. It was a high-wing monoplane driven by four propellers. Pilots said that it was a very easy aeroplane to fly. The cargo hold was large enough to take a three-ton lorry or fifty

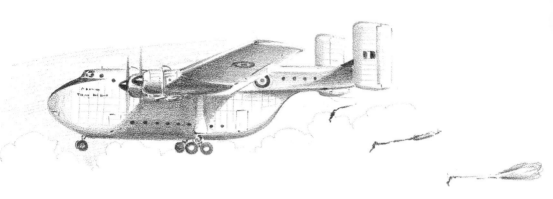

soldiers. Upstairs from the cargo hold was the boom that joined the tail assembly to the rest of the aircraft. The boom in fact was almost as big as the fuselage of a Hastings and held, if I remember correctly, twenty soldiers with their equipment. At the back end of the boom, set in the floor, was a door that hinged upwards and sideways in two halves, to leave a hole about four feet wide and six feet long.

To jump, one stood at the forward edge of the hole facing aft, and simply took one pace forwards into thin air. The effect was wonderful. One moment I was standing in an aeroplane, next instant I was outside it, sitting in an airy armchair as the slipstream closed up around my body. For a couple of seconds I sat there as on a cushion of compressed air, looking back along the aeroplane's track and watching the parachutists who had already gone out in various stages of development. The first out would be furthest away, his canopy fully developed. Number two's canopy would be a crumpled dome still filling with air. Number three's canopy would be pulling out of its bag, while my own rigging lines were still paying out. It only lasted for two or three seconds, but in this time every detail would imprint itself in my memory.

I also enjoyed the ride down under the open parachute canopy. Sitting up there, comfortably held by the harness, one felt a sense of detachment. Riding down under my canopy, I could look along the line of parachutes swaying to and fro and watch the other parachutists lowering their weapons containers, pulling on lift webs to damp out oscillation, or steering away from too-close neighbours. I wasn't too keen on landings, having been battered on many occasions due to my poor landing technique. Nevertheless, I liked parachuting and being up there in the sky. So I suppose it was inevitable that I should want to take up free-fall parachuting.

What better place to go to learn this exciting skill than to Netheravon in Wiltshire, where the Army Parachute Association had its free-fall school.

Up to this time I had been an active military parachutist for fifteen years, less injury time. Like all members of the Parachute Regiment, both Regular and Territorial, I reckoned I was a cut above ordinary men and knew a thing or two about parachuting as well. After all, I had started in the days before reserve parachutes were worn. At Netheravon I learned how little I knew.

I was cut down to size in the nicest possible way by Don Hughes and his excellent staff. They were firm, friendly, competent and dedicated. The atmosphere was informal and relaxed. I liked the place immediately. Students were accepted from both regular and territorial forces and two places were reserved on each course for civilians. At the weekends all sorts of parachutists, civilian and military, male and female, would turn up at the school to jump.

The Novices' Free-Fall Course started as all good courses should with a talk by the Chief Instructor, Don Hughes. Then we learned how to pack our own parachutes, how they worked, how to put them on and how to control them in the air. We practised landing rolls on the mats in the ground training room. We learned how to climb aboard the De Havilland Rapide aeroplane and how to get out of it in flight, cleanly and without fuss.

This occupied the first three days of the course. On the fourth day we were practising packing our parachutes for the umpteenth time on the long packing tables in the packing room. Most of us had finished packing and were gossiping, well satisfied with our efforts, our packed 'chutes lying on the tables beside us. An instructor walked in. "All packed are you? Good! You'll be using them this afternoon. First jump of the course at 1400!"

We all looked at each other. Then as one man we all without exception pulled our ripcord handles, shook out our canopies and began a very, very careful packing. This time it was for real! No parachutes were ever more carefully packed.

The first three jumps at the school were made with the parachute operated by an eight-feet-long webbing static line which opened the pack as the parachutist fell away from the aeroplane in the spreadeagled free-fall position known as a "stable spread". These three static line jumps were simply to get used to exiting from the aircraft and holding a good stable spread position.

The next three jumps were also on the static line. But for these jumps one

had to pull a dummy ripcord handle from its elasticated pocket on the left shoulder strap of the harness. Then as one fell clear of the aircraft, one showed it to the despatcher in the departing aeroplane.

My first descent went off without incident. On my second jump I landed off the airfield among a herd of cows. They rushed up, eager and curious to see this intruder from the sky, and started pawing at the precious nylon of my parachute canopy. I rushed back at them, shouting and waving my arms, and they retreated a few paces. I gathered in a few armfuls of nylon and shooed them off again. Gradually I backed up to the electric fence and stepped very carefully over it, remembering as I did so an extremely painful experience some years before in Germany. On that occasion, at dead of night on a Nato exercise, my thin combat trousers soaking wet, I had crossed a similar wire. At the critical moment my feet had slipped in the mud and I had done the splits over the wire and sat astride it for an instant before my electrified body had reacted and catapulted me into the air.

On my fourth static line descent I miscalculated my approach to the landing area on the field. With absolute horror I realised that I was going to land backwards on the roof of one of the hangars. So I did the only safe thing in the circumstances; I turned my canopy till I was facing downwind. Then driving with the wind, the air pouring out of the slots in the back of the canopy and driving it forwards, I sailed over the threatening roof until the curl-over of air on the downwind side of the building smashed me downwards to the ground with such force that the stitching of the yellow terylene strap holding my reserve parachute flat against my waist snapped. The reserve pack then bounced upwards, pivoting on the D rings that secured it to the main harness, and struck me on the nose, drawing a plentiful stream of blood from both nostrils and from the gash on the outside of my nose.

The static line jumps were nevertheless all judged to be satisfactory. I was to go on to my first free fall, a delay of five seconds before opening my parachute.

A parachutist's first free-fall parachute jump is a unique occasion. This is the first time that he has jumped from the security of the aeroplane with his fate entirely in his own hands. He can choose to pull the ripcord or not to pull it. He can make a clean pull or a hopeless mess. One thing is certain: one's first free fall is something special, it only happens once, and it will never be forgotten.

When the great day arrived for me, I packed my parachute with extra special care. I paid particular attention to the fit of the four ripcord pins in the cones that held the pack shut. I made sure that the ripcord handle was properly stowed in its elasticated pocket. Then, donning my parachute, I carefully adjusted the harness to a comfortable fit, a fraction here, a touch there. I clipped my reserve onto the front of the harness, picked up my Everoak crash helmet and walked out of the packing room into the bright September sunshine. I joined five other men to make up the plane-load of six. The aeroplane would make two runs over the airfield, dropping three men on each run.

We climbed aboard and sat on the floor. I felt very tense and dry-mouthed. The instructor took his seat by the door, and the Rapide with a great revving of her engines trundled and bumped across the grass until she was airborne. She lifted herself into the air and passed low over the gravel pit used as a target for accuracy jumps. Then she was over the Amesbury–Marlborough road and turning left in a great circle that would take her up to 2300 feet.

On the bulkhead behind the instructor there was an altimeter. I watched its white finger creeping slowly round the dial. The instructor caught my eye and grinned at me. I smiled back. Then the instructor leaned out of the door, looking at some distant point ahead. His right hand reached up and pressed one of the white push buttons at the top of the door frame. The aeroplane immediately swung a few degrees to the right in a flat turn. The instructor seemed to be satisfied. He was watching the ground. Then he pressed the centre button and gestured to us first three men to stand up. Looking at me, he pointed through the open door at the wing.

I climbed out into the slipstream, felt it against my face, saw it rippling my green overall sleeve as I reached for the interplane strut. I felt a tap on my right arm, the signal to go, and I was gone. I spread my arms and legs out in the stable spread, arched my back till it was hollow, and looked up at the aeroplane in time to see the next man climbing out onto the wing. As I fell I was counting out the seconds. In the first second I had fallen only sixteen feet. By the end of the second second I had fallen through sixty-two feet. By the end of the five seconds I would have fallen a total of three hundred and

sixty-six feet. On the count of "four" I brought my right hand in to grasp the ripcord handle, while at the same time my left arm moved into place above my head to centralise the lift provided by the resistance of my left hand against the rushing air.

On the count of "five" I pulled the ripcord handle and spread both arms again. I felt the restraining tug of the harness at my shoulders and as my body jerked into an upright position I knew that I had made a good, stable delay. I was pleased with myself.

I looked up and beamed at my canopy. I grinned to myself all the way down to the airfield. I made a perfect landing. With pounding exhilaration within my chest, I roughly field-packed my parachute, clipped it to my reserve and hoisted both parachutes over my shoulder. Then I walked lightly over the grass to the Chief Instructor for de-briefing.

"If you do that again," said the CI, "you'll be off the course and I'll ground you for six months."

"What . . .?" I managed to gasp.

"You delayed for seven seconds before pulling. If you over-run your time again, you're out."

I walked away, crestfallen, my ego cut down to size.

Netheravon was such a wonderful place that one couldn't be down-hearted for long. The drive and enthusiasm of Don Hughes carried us all along on the course. In two and a half weeks the novices' course progressed in steps of three jumps from the static line jumps through three descents of five seconds free-fall delay, three ten-second delays, to three fifteen-second delays.

Interspersed with the jumps there were lectures and informal chats on the theory of free fall parachuting. We listened to these with the utmost attention to make sure that we understood. Once the parachutist has leaped from the aeroplane he is completely on his own. If he hasn't learned what to do by then, he has left it just a little too late. Surprisingly, instructions and explanations that had been heard but once only would be remembered at the critical moment.

I was on the brink of instability – aerodynamic instability. My spread-eagled, cruciform body was at 3000 feet and falling fast. I had felt the airspeed building up, heard the wind note rising in my helmet, felt the air getting stiffer. My outflung arms and legs were riding the wind. Then my body started buffeting, a to-and-fro movement. Suddenly I was falling. I was no longer flying, riding the cushion of compressed air that supports the stable free-fall parachutist. This was different. I was falling and about to topple over. I began to roll over onto my right side. All my instincts screamed at me to put out my right hand and push down on the air to stop myself tumbling over. Then that ice-cold feeling that seems to take over control of one's thinking in an emergency came to the rescue and my memory retrieved a phrase I had once heard: "Put on the arch."

I had heard the phrase one day when walking past a group of students on the airfield at Netheravon. They were gathered around an instructor, Bob Acraman, who was speaking informally on matters aerodynamic. I stopped, listened and became enthralled. Acraman was explaining the aerodynamics of free fall. Sitting comfortably on the low roof of the fuel bunker, he looked down at us in the sunshine and spoke of stability, buffeting, lift, turning, spinning and controlling a flying human body. Sixty minutes passed in the conscious space of six. He was explaining stability in the air and why it was necessary to stick out the tummy and hollow the back to present a rounded surface to the rushing air. "You must have a good arch," he was saying. "Arch your back and make it hollow." Then he had described the warning symptoms of instability and how to combat them, ". . . and all you have to do is put on the arch."

"Put on the arch!" It spun off the memory circuits into my conscious thinking. Nerves carried the message, muscles moved. I actually heard again the voice saying, "Put on the arch!" My brain over-rode my reflex instincts. The hand that was reaching down to press on the air shot upwards as my spine arched backwards. "Put on the arch!" and to my surprise, it worked. Stability was restored.

We learned much from our instructors at Netheravon, sometimes in

formal lectures, sometimes through informal chats, and they were always ready to answer our questions. They taught us how to turn our freely falling bodies through 360 degrees, and how to stop the turn at any desired point. We learned how to control and get out of a spin, how to control buffeting and how to deal with a ripcord handle that refuses to pull. They showed us how to steer our parachutes and how to control the descent so as to land where we wanted to. They showed us how to pack our parachutes. They opened up a whole new world of experience to us. All these and many other things we learned from our instructors at Netheravon. We stored them away in our memories, ready for the emergency when we might want to remember a phrase like "Put on the arch!"

At Netheravon I enjoyed the purest form of flight of which man is capable. It is the ultimate experience. Leave me there, surrounded by air, bathed in sunshine, flying over the green fields of Wiltshire.

8

A SLIGHT MISCALCULATION

I was visiting Netheravon again. I had planned to stay for a week of my holidays and enjoy some parachuting. Now on my second day I was in hospital — Tidworth Military Hospital. It was my second serious parachuting injury. I had made a fifteen-second free-fall delay and been briefed to make a 360-degree turn before opening my parachute. Just before I jumped out of the Rapide the despatcher had asked me, "Which way will you make the turn?"

"To the right," I replied, climbing out onto the lower port wing and reaching out a hand for the interplane strut. Then I was gone.

I felt the air stiffen, knew again the old exhilaration of being out in the sky alone, unsupported, and saw the Rapide disappear upwards. Then I picked my datum on the horizon and started the turn. Salisbury Plain revolved 4000 feet beneath me. Then it stopped. I tried to restart the turn. Salisbury Plain remained static. Puzzled, I leaned on the air, forcing my body to the right. Suddenly I felt my back muscles give. My body flopped. I hastily pulled the handle and winced at the shock. I hung in my harness like a rag doll, knowing that something dreadful had happened inside me. I landed in a heap and knelt on the ground for several minutes, still, painful, hoping that what I knew was not true. I had no desire to stand up. Very slowly, on my knees, I field-packed my 'chute. Then I staggered to my feet, straight-backed, and slowly, stiffly, walked off the field with my load.

That afternoon I rested in my room and had a very hot bath. I took another bath in the evening and went to bed early. In the morning I awoke and tried to get up. I found that I couldn't. I lay still as the panic gripped at my throat and brain. Then I forced an arm to move. Sandpaper rasped inside my back muscles. I moved a leg and tried to sit up in bed. Impossible. Breathing heavily, sweating, afraid, I lay still and worked out a plan.

If I could get my right arm under me and cross my left leg over my right leg I might be able to roll over onto the edge of the bed and lower my feet to the floor. Slowly I moved my left leg. Inch by inch, carefully, I reached the edge of the bed and eased the covers aside. Then I rolled over the edge, almost screamed, and ended up kneeling at the side of the bed. I stayed there for twenty minutes before I had either the strength or the will to pull myself up to a standing position. Eventually, by will power and good navigation, I arrived in the bathroom and soaked in a hot bath.

By midday even my optimism had run out and I carefully lowered myself into my car and drove at twenty mph to Tidworth Military Hospital. I had been there before for treatment of minor injuries, and the sister who admitted me smiled and remarked, ''Hallo! It's you again!''

In the ward was a mixed bag of regular officers. The bed next to me was occupied by a cheerful major. The other patients were a Royal Engineer captain, an infantry subaltern, a Captain RN, and an officer who was soon to die.

Three beds away lived the Captain RN, who made a point of never speaking to soldiers unless he had to. Perhaps he disliked us. He was a bulky, middle-aged man with sparse grey hair. From time to time he would get up and stomp along the verandah, to and fro. "I see the Captain's walking his bridge again," said the cheerful major.

I was X-rayed and prodded and questioned. Finally, with great authority, a full colonel in the RAMC told me what I already knew — that I had torn my back muscles, two layers of them. There was apparently a third layer still intact and this had enabled me to walk.

Trolleys clattered, nurses came and went, pills, bed pans, bed baths, sleep, wakefulness, pain, Captain walking his bridge, physiotherapy, and so it went on and on.

Late one afternoon the officer whose life had been ebbing away died quietly, without fuss, and the body that had contained him was removed. Next day the military admin machine would move smoothly through the procedures prescribed for such an occurrence.

When I had nothing else to do, I would set my brain to Random Access and wait to see what it would retrieve from its memory banks. The time was 22.00. The night sister had said "Good night", the lights were out save for a small lamp in the corner. The after-glow of the sunset persisted in a water-colour sky. It was at this very hour some years ago that I had stood in a balloon cage suspended 700 feet above the racecourse (the Roodee) at Chester.

The wind had been strong that night and it shook and flapped and whistled at the fabric roof of the cage. Chester Military Tattoo was in full swing below on the grass at the centre of the course. A mock battle was in progress. The six men in the balloon cage watched the flashes and heard the explosions. We saw the defenders of the bunker pinned down with covering fire from the Bren group, saw the rifle sections run behind the Bren gun to new, nearer positions from which they could assault with the bayonet. Then the battle was over, the goodies had won and the baddies were killed or taken prisoner.

The arena was cleared and we six parachutists waited expectantly, keyed up, nervous, a little apprehensive of the tearing, tossing wind that clattered around the canvas and rigging. With a brilliant white glare, a searchlight swung up and caught and held the tail of the balloon in a bright shimmer of silver set in the dark night sky. The despatcher unhooked and dropped aside the bar. Number one stepped forward, stood poised for a moment in the open door space silhouetted against the glare, and then jumped out into the night. The searchlight locked onto his canopy and seemed to guide him to a safe landing in the centre of the arena. A pink rippling was suddenly visible all around the edge of the racecourse and we five watchers in the balloon recognised it as applause. Number two steadied himself in the door and was gone an instant later. More pink applause.

Then it was my turn. I waited in the door for the searchlight beam to swing up again. It illuminated the great tail fins of the balloon and picked out sharply the spiral twist of the tethering ropes that hung down on either side of the tail, occasionally lashing in the wind. Then I heard the despatcher's "Go!" and I leaped out forcibly, driving hard. My canopy was white and in the searchlight's glare it glistened and sparkled and moved with little undulations and ripples and seemed to be alive. I reached up and grasped the lift webs, glanced over my shoulder to ensure that I was descending clear of the balloon cable (marked at 100-foot intervals by little red and white socks) and settled down to make a good approach to the centre of the Roodee as the previous two parachutists had done. Ahead lay the city of Chester with its roof tops, and its street lamps. To the right lay the silver curve of the River Dee. Below me the grass of the arena sparkled and glittered in the criss-crossing beams of the searchlights.

But something was wrong! I was drifting over the heads of the spectators! Now I was flying over the red roofs of the pavilions. I was out over the road. A grey slate roof passed astern. Buildings with hard, sharp roofs lay awaiting me. There were dark bottomless shadows containing Heaven knew what leg-breaking obstacles. I was alarmed, very alarmed. I was now at 200 feet and oscillating to and fro as the wind lifted and swirled around the buildings below. I reached up and pulled down hard on a rear lift web until I was grasping the rigging lines. I wasn't alarmed any more – I was desperate! The roofs began to recede. Then there was only one tall Victorian roof between me and safety. I lifted my legs and skimmed over it. Then I was over the road and coming in fast. I landed on cobblestones at the foot of a tree. A female voice exclaimed, "My, you did come down with a bang!"

Seven hundred feet above the earth in the balloon cage, the despatcher turned to the remaining parachutists and said, "The bloody fool! He was pulling on the wrong lift webs!"

9

A WING OF MY OWN

My parachuting days were nearly over. But I didn't know this and so I bought a parachute. She was twenty-eight feet in diameter and I paid thirty pounds for her at the free-fall school at Netheravon. She was a brand-new C9 canopy divided into four segments of orange, green, white and brown ripstop nylon, housed in a secondhand cotton sleeve bearing the name ''Don Hughes'' written with a black ballpoint pen. The canopy, sleeve and single extractor 'chute were contained within a bluish-green B4 back-pack.

She was beautifully engineered, a joy to see and a pleasure to touch. Her firm webbing harness was secured to my body with three D-rings. Her canopy, soft slithery nylon, had been modified by a sergeant instructor at the school to a 9-gore elliptical TU configuration. This meant that material had been cut away from the back of the canopy in the shape of two inverted T's joined together by their cross bars, thus ⊥⊥ , the whole modification cutting across nine gores, and the cross-bar cut in an elliptical shape. This was the most powerful modification that one could cut into a C9 canopy, giving it a forward speed in still air of up to ten knots. In the air, fully inflated, she flew steadily with little oscillation, and the sunlight striking her upper surface made her alive with light when seen from below. Her ripcord, a stainless steel stranded wire with four chromium-plated pins that locked the four cones holding the pack closed, passed through a stainless steel flexible tube from the top of her pack to the left-hand side of her harness where the handle rested in an elasticated pocket.

With careful adjustment of buckles she had been made to fit my lean frame comfortably, giving me a sense of well-being and security whenever I fastened her about me.

Her short career lasted but three months. It started on the day following my fortieth birthday. For this, her maiden flight, and because I had not jumped for over six months, she was fitted with a static line that would automatically open her pack as I made my exit off the wing of the old

Rapide. At an altitude of 2500 feet I leaped gently backwards and reached for the dummy ripcord handle that had been substituted for the real handle when the static line had been fitted. Finding it at the first attempt, I removed it and waved it at the despatcher looking backwards at me from the ever-open door of the receding Rapide.

My log book records, "2500, SL, dummy pull, wind 5 mph. Fair — left hand not far enough over during the pull." But I didn't care at that moment that my technique during the pull had left much to be desired. I was looking intently upwards, watching the development of my new partner. She streamed from the sleeve, threw her skirt to the wind and billowed out. Then, as most parachutes will, she partially collapsed (it's called "breathing") before firmly inflating herself and bearing me down to a soft landing on the green grass airfield that is Netheravon.

During subsequent jumps I made free-fall delays of up to fifteen seconds before pulling her ripcord and each time I noted how gentle was her opening as she enveloped the air that was to bear us down to the earth again. I got to know her flying qualities, how she turned, how quickly she would stop a turn, her rate of descent, and how long she would hold herself facing into wind without any corrective tugs on her steering toggles.

Sometimes I would leave her to her own devices and she, sensing my mood, would weathercock until, with her back to the wind and the air driving out of her slots, we would race away downwind, chasing our shadow on the grass below, deliberately ignoring the commands of the CI's loud-hailer on the ground urging us to "Turn into wind now". Then at the last possible moment I would gently pull down on one of her steering toggles and she would turn easily till she was facing into wind again. Giving me just enough time to assess my drift and turn my feet accordingly, she would set me gently down before she subsided gracefully onto the grass beside me.

Sometimes in an impish mood, assisted by a stronger wind, she would let me rise to my feet after landing and then she would pull and drag me protesting across the airfield, to the delight and cheers of my fellows.

Sometimes I would pull her ripcord early, seconds before I needed to, so that we would have a longer flight together. I would pull down strongly on one steering toggle and the deformation of one of her vertical slots would shoot the air out at a tangent and she would rotate. I would keep pulling down hard so that we both went round like a merry-go-round, centrifugal force throwing me outwards from her canopy. And sometimes, riding the fickle wind, we would find ourselves over the hangars, fighting hard to reach a clear space free of obstructions where she could set me safely down.

On other occasions we would try for a precision spot landing in the centre of the great gravel pit used in competitions. We would watch other parachutists below us and weave S-turns to lose height without overshooting. We would drive down the wind gradient in grand style, and once we actually managed to land somewhere near the pit.

As I gathered her up after each descent I would admire again the quality of her stitching and the dependable engineering of her harness. I loved the smooth, sensual softness of her nylon canopy. I would carry her into the packing room and carefully pleat her canopy, fourteen folds to the left and fourteen folds to the right. Then I would draw down the sleeve to encase the canopy and begin the task of stowing her rigging lines in the elastics. After that would come the battle to persuade her into her pack. She always resisted strenuously at this stage, but eventually the last pin would be pushed home in its cone and she would be ready for another descent.

10

LAST JUMP

The end came on a warm, sunny September day, a day of blue sky, fluffy cumulus and a gentle breeze, a day made for parachuting. I had been briefed to make a fifteen-second free-fall delay in the course of which I was to make a 360-degree turn. It was to be my hundredth jump. During the hour of waiting beforehand I felt uneasy and visited the toilet four times. I knew that in some way this would be a notable jump. (Can the person, the man himself, foretell danger to the body that houses him?) I boarded the aircraft and settled myself on the hard wooden flooring with five other parachutists.

The Rapide reached 4200 feet. The despatcher motioned me to my feet (there are no words of command at Netheravon – gestures are less likely to be misunderstood). Then with a pointing-out-of-the-door gesture the despatcher ordered me out of the aircraft.

As I climbed out through the door of the biplane I heard my brain whispering, "Left hand, left leg", and my limbs, long accustomed to blind obedience to training, reached out for the interplane strut as I stepped out onto the small black rubber pad glued to the top surface of the lower wing. I stood on the wing for a few seconds, clinging to the diagonal strut from which the sweaty grasp of many hands had rubbed away the dark blue paint down to the green undercoat. I was aware of the propeller wash tearing at me and rippling rapidly along the sleeves of my overalls.

Then I passed irrevocably through the moment of decision. Leaping gently backwards, I extended my arms and gave myself up to the wonder of human flight.

I waited a few seconds to pick up speed and feel the air stiffen on my hands, those sensitive control surfaces that would guide me into the turn I was about to make. Selecting a wooded feature on the horizon as a datum, I began the turn. The earth rotated below me. It was as though I was stationary in space and the landscape moved in response to the movement of my hands and the inclining of my body. The horizon tilted as it rotated and I watched it, fascinated. Woodlands went by, moving from right to left. The Marlborough–Amesbury road passed by, followed by the sweep of land out to Boscombe Down. Then I had completed my turn and Salisbury Plain was back in place again. I stabilised myself on my original heading and the land stopped rotating. My datum was now myself. I was isolated, detached from everything else. Suspended in complete self-sufficiency above the earth, I was dependent only on myself and God.

With every second now that passed I flew through 174 feet of altitude, the wind noise a steady roar in my helmet. As the count of "fifteen" came up on that metronome in my brain I reached in, grasped and pulled the ripcord handle, and awaited the gentle tugging at my shoulders that would pull me upright beneath my canopy. Instead I heard a muffled bang. There was a violent jerk.

I looked up and without thinking I said aloud, "A bundle of washing," for that was exactly what it looked like – no longer the perfect form of an inflated canopy but just a bundle of washing shot through with holes. The rigging lines were hopelessly tangled and twisted and the whole mass, including me, rotated about once every five seconds.

I contemplated it for a while. Then I looked at the ground still a long way below me, too far below to enable me to estimate my rate of descent. I looked up and searched the sky for other parachutists. As I rotated I saw two other canopies both apparently moving upwards at a considerable speed. With genuine reluctance I placed my left hand over the flaps of my reserve parachute while my right hand pulled the reserve handle out and placed it between my teeth. Carefully letting the elastics pull aside the flaps of the reserve, I grasped the ball of white nylon that was the reserve canopy and threw it strongly in the direction of rotation. It vanished from sight. I had just time to say, "Oh God, it's gone," when it suddenly inflated as I rotated to meet it.

I was rather surprised and somewhat pleased at the smoothness with which I had carried out the drill for flying my reserve. Then I noticed that it, too, had partially malfunctioned. The rigging lines had twisted together for about a third of their length and were pulling the reserve canopy into a sphere with its bottom cut off, rather than holding it as a hemisphere. I tried unsuccessfully to untwist the lines. Then moving the reserve handle from between my teeth, I waited for the landing.

I came in fast and tore the ligaments of my right foot. I stood up, ripped the crash helmet from my head and hurled it at the ground at the same time shouting an obscene and unprintable word at the top of my voice. The Chief Instructor drove over in a Land Rover and inspected both canopies which I had been careful not to disturb. "Are you all right?" he asked, and didn't bat an eyelid at my reply. Both parachutes were bundled aboard the Land Rover and with their owner were driven off the DZ. Throughout the entire incident I had the detached feeling of standing aside and watching it all happen. My only emotion was a cold-blooded interest in watching myself doing what I was doing.

Some months later I re-visited Netheravon. I limped through the tall drying room with its multicoloured canopies draped from the ceiling, past the rows of metal shelves holding students' parachutes ready packed for use, and into the parachute repair workshop. There was a large cardboard box on the floor in a corner of the room. In it was a canopy, orange, green, white and brown. I raised an enquiring eyebrow and the sergeant instructor nodded. Silently I picked up a pair of scissors and cut out a strip of orange nylon. Wrapping it around my neck in the manner of a scarf, I limped out into the sunshine of Netheravon.

I visited Netheravon about a year later. My foot was healed and I wanted to jump again. On that occasion the wind was too strong for parachuting. I came again a month later. This time cloud base was too low: no jumping. I wandered over to the hangars. All were locked except for one that I had never been in before. It was full of gliders. I recognised a man sandpapering a wing on one of the aircraft as General Deane-Drummond, whom I had met some years previously. We spoke of gliding, or rather he did. He let me examine his machine. I looked at all the others as well.

Next day when I returned home, I didn't want to admit it, even to myself, but I knew that my parachuting days were over.

11

NEW WINGS

What should I do next? There had been excitement, joy and satisfaction in parachuting, in being up there above the earth. Even though I was still a novice, falling freely, unsupported through the air, a whole new and rewarding mental and physical experience had been opened up for me. I had to get back into the air again. Perhaps gliding would satisfy. I thought over my conversation with Deane Drummond in the hangar at Netheravon and decided to go on a week's gliding course. I chose the Midland Gliding Club at the Long Mynd in Shropshire. By the end of the course I could control the two-seater glider up the launch on the end of the long winch cable that pulled us up into the sky like a kite. I could steer it on a somewhat uncertain course and turn it to left and right. But land it I could not! Even as a parachutist, landings were not my strong point and I had bruises to prove it!

After the course I joined the Blackpool and Fylde Gliding Club, which was based neither at Blackpool nor at Fylde, but at Samlesbury. Slowly my flying technique improved until two years later I made my first solo flight. Up to this time my training had been in a side-by-side two-seater glider. Now, for my first solo flight, I was to transfer to a single-seat glider known as the Eon Baby (Eon for Elliots of Newbury, the manufacturers). The Eon was quite small, had an open cockpit with small windscreen, and the wings were held in place by struts, one on each side of the fuselage.

I can remember very little about my first solo flight. I do recall flying up the launch in this unfamiliar narrow cockpit, and I know that the landing was so smooth that I was uncertain for a few seconds as to whether or not I had actually touched the tarmac runway. My outstanding impression is of Chief Flying Instructor Jack Aked's pleasure that another pupil had gone solo. When the Eon came to a stop he ran up to me, clutching the field glasses through which he had observed my flight. His face beamed with pleasure and his moustache quivered with the excitement of the occasion.

I made three flights in the Eon Baby that day, which began a new love-hate relationship, for she could be very contrary. But as her new pilot came to know her, she would carry him up to where the wind whispered. And sometimes the wind would blow in over the side and warn him that he was side-slipping. When she flew at the correct speed the wind would whisper

quietly of flights to come, and her pilot would be relaxed and drained of all his tensions.

Throughout the year the Eon would carry her pilots free at last from the restraint of the voice in the left-hand seat. She would force them to make their own decisions and thereby become better pilots. Weekend after weekend she would take her pilots sometimes to the left and sometimes to the right of a circuit of the airfield, each circuit revealing something new in her handling, or in the sky, or in the landscape below. Sometimes, with one more skilled than the rest, she would explore the higher regions of the air, and the Lancashire landscape would spread out until on the one hand it vanished into the silvery-grey sheen of the sea, and on the other it merged with distant cloud banks in a rim of man-made haze until it joined with the limitless sky in making up the Eon's world. Then she would tire of her partner (for she was a fickle creature) and her altimeter needle would unwind until she had settled herself once more upon the runways of Samlesbury and she would await another's hand on her stick and his feet pressing her pedals.

She was contrary, exciting, exasperating, frightening and soothing. She gave to us who first soloed in her our first taste of aerial independence. She heard us curse and pray. She heard us shout and sing and whistle. But, good mistress that she was, she never betrayed one lover to another and each thought that she was for him alone. She was the sort of glider that one either loved or hated.

12

THE SKY IS NEUTRAL

As time went by and I progressed from the Eon Baby to gliders of better performance and enclosed cockpits, I began to think of myself as a glider pilot. My parachutist days slipped away into the background of memory. It was a good thing to have done. Now it was past.

Eventually I became a part-owner of the Eon Baby, that infuriating glider on which I had soloed. Now that I was a more competent pilot it was a pleasure once again to fly the little Eon. With no restricting perspex canopy, my head once again out in the air, I began really to enjoy the sky again. With the other members of the Eon syndicate I joined the Vintage Glider Club of Great Britain and a whole new world of gliding opened up for me; I discovered that for a parachutist turned glider pilot there was still magic in the sky.

Frank Searle called it "the crowded sky" and wrote a book about it. Other authors have taken the opposite view and described it as "vast", "limitless", "great cavern of the sky", "enormous bowl of heaven" and so on, searching for words and phrases to convey the immeasurable size, the vast emptiness of the sky. The truth of the matter is that the sky is a great paradox. It is both large and small. It all depends on where we are and on what we are doing. The sky is neutral. It will let us lose ourselves in peaceful solitude. It will provide space for flying training exercises. It will allow us to fly great distances. It will provide the vast spaces that release the poet, the writer, the romantic in the pilot. It will provide one small space, one precise co-ordinate at which to die. The pilot makes the decisions. The sky remains neutral.

I had never seriously thought about this until I was gliding in France at the 6th International Vintage Glider Rally. The Vintage Internationals, the brain-child of Chris Wills, the President of the Vintage Glider Club of Great Britain, are held annually in a different country each year. They are good, happy, sociable occasions with plenty of flying for the vintage gliders and their vintage pilots. The daily briefings at these rallies are given in German, French and English, and the serious business of the weather forecast, flight safety, availability of tugs and winches is always interspersed with good humour and laughter.

On this occasion I sat in the cockpit of the Eon Baby and watched the silver, parasol-winged Morane-Saulnier with its big black radial engine taxi towards me on the great flat airfield at Brienne-le-Château. As it turned broadside on, I held my hand above my head with four fingers outstretched to request a towing speed of 80 kilometres per hour. The tug pilot acknowledged with a curt nod of his head and turned the Morane into wind. The tow-rope was hooked onto the rear of the tug. My pre-take-off nerves churned and my diaphragm tightened. As the tug's engine roared and it moved slowly forward to take up the slack in the rope, the nervous tension vanished as though it had never been there and left me and my glider as an extension of the tug pilot. Wherever he went we would follow.

The roar of the Morane's engine deepened and the two aircraft moved slowly forward, accelerating gently along the grass strip at the side of the long concrete runway where the tugs landed. The rumbling of the wheel stopped and the Eon Baby skimmed the ground at an altitude of two feet. The crosswind from the left pushed the glider over to the right of the tug. I worked the rudder pedals, my eyes fixed on the silver aeroplane still rumbling along the grass in front of me. Would it never fly? How much longer in this crosswind? The wind from the left pushed the Eon still further to the right of the tug. Get off the ground, you ancient silver crock! I was now looking over the cockpit side at the tug aircraft. Holding the wings level with ailerons and pressing on a little more rudder, I wondered whether or not to pull off the tow-rope. Time seemed to stretch on and on. I knew that it was less than half a minute since the start of the tow but subjective time stretched and extended till it seemed that I had been in this crosswind for ever. The Morane roared on like some badly designed ground vehicle, its wings waggling as it hit bumps on the grass strip. How much longer in this crosswind? The old, underpowered rattletrap lumbered on, the Eon following, skewed at an angle as the wind tried to push it off to the right. Then the Morane lifted up into a cobalt-blue sky. The Eon lagged a little, then with a gentle backwards movement of the stick rose up and held the beautifully proportioned silver aeroplane just below the horizon.

Time slipped backwards. The silver aeroplane with the black radial engine and the parasol wing had been designed in 1930 when I was a boy and

the Eon Baby did not exist. The landscape, the woods, the lakes, fields, sky and the parasol aeroplane were all the same as they were in those distant pre-war days when I had declared to my parents that I was going to be an aeroplane driver. The Morane would have been the latest thing in light aircraft on that sunny Empire Day in 1930 when my father took me to the air display and the R 101 flew over. My father held me up to look into the cockpits of the silver biplanes that smelt of doped fabric and oil, and I heard the sounds of piston engines, the same sound as wafted back to me now that I was a man, physically here but mentally there back in the 'thirties, physically tied by the tow-rope to that reminder of the past that was now straining up into the vast, enormous spaces of the present-day sky. All the while some small part of me was flying through a 1930s sky, untroubled by the present, an escape route, a refuge in a safe past.

Then irritating, annoying instinct started nagging, sounding its warnings within the brain. "The sky is a small place," it said. "Look out." My eyes observed a sky bounded only at its lower surface by the earth. "It has limited flight paths," remarked instinct. The hot July sky appeared to be limitless. "They fly too close to you," continued instinct. I raised my eyes from the tug aircraft and searched overhead and to each side. Nothing there. Another quick look around. Nothing. The clash between instinct and intellect at times creates an uneasy feeling at the back of one's head. I glanced back at the tug. We were out of position. The tug appeared to be too high and to the left.

I eased back a fraction on the stick and pressed gently on the left rudder pedal. The tug appeared to move back into position. A glance at the ASI showed 42 knots. The tug slowly turned to the right. I pointed the Eon's nose at the tug's left wing-tip and we both went round as on a railway track, the Eon a perfect extension of the Morane's control stick and rudder pedals. At 42 knots I could clearly hear the roar of the radial engine above the hiss of air as it rushed past my own aircraft, dragging and swirling around its unstreamlined vintage form. The air parted to let the blunt nose, with its aerotow hook stuck out in front, pass by as the slightly bowed tow-rope

dragged it through yet more air which divided either side of the struts that held the thick wings against the upthrust of the lifting stream of air eddying and flowing in the wake of the glider.

From time to time the instinct of self-preservation broke through my concentration and my eyes swept the sky to both sides and above. Meanwhile reason insisted that there was nothing to worry about – the tug pilot was in command. At 1500 feet or thereabouts, the Morane rocked its silver, ribbed, parasol wing and I pulled the yellow release knob on the left of the matt black instrument panel. As the Morane dived for the earth I circled to the right and searched for the airfield, found it and relaxed a little. (I will never, as long as I live, forget how I lost Münster-Telgte when a German tug pilot waved me off in sink, out of sight of the airfield.) As I continued the turn I caught a glimpse of the Morane still diving down, the sun glinting off its silver wing's upper surface, a magic, frozen image of a vanished past, now permanently preserved in that marvellous faculty we call memory.

The thermal took the glider slowly up in weak lift into a blue, almost cloudless sky. Three other gliders joined in and suddenly brain and instinct were in accord – the sky *is* a small place. The Eon circled in a narrow radius, with the other three gliders carving great circles around it. At 28 knots the Eon slowly gained height and I began to take a deeper interest in the other three machines circling like sharks.

I glanced at the red piece of string streaming back from the pitot tube. The variometer showed two feet per second up. The three sharks still circled around the little yellow Eon. We climbed past the 2000-feet mark in brilliant sunshine, the light glancing and flashing from the wings and fuselages of the other machines. Another instrument scan showed 2200 feet, a fraction over two feet per second, and the red string fairly central, wobbling about in the slipstream.

Outside the security of the Eon's cockpit the two sharks still circled around. Two? Where was the third? Above? No, not above! Then behind? Yes, there it was, a white shape keeping perfect station behind the Eon. Fool! It's your own tailplane! Where is it then? The vast sky had suddenly become a narrow vertical funnel containing an Eon Baby at its centre, two other gliders that could be seen, and one unseen enemy who could be anywhere, and perhaps couldn't see the Eon Baby. Strange how the brain transfers values. The unseen glider had progressed from 'glider' to 'shark' to 'enemy'. The narrow, treacherous, aerial funnel continued upwards with the Eon flanked by the other two in a close company that demanded the utmost in concentration. The sky had closed in to a slim vertical cylinder.

At 2800 feet I lost the thermal and in an instant the sky was empty. The three sharks had vanished. The vast, unlimited blue was as undisturbed as if no machine other than the little Eon Baby had ever flown through its quiet, still air. The sky stretched in all directions with only one small yellow

vintage glider meandering here and there on its way to the solid security of the earth. The dark greens of the woodlands, the yellows and light browns of the crops, the light varied greens of the pastures, all stretched away until the colours mingled, softened and blended into the distance where the horizon merged with a continuous line that was neither earth nor sky. Then suddenly, a white object closed rapidly from head on and shot by in the small confines of the tight, close, compressed sky no more than fifty metres away on the left and vanished astern as the Eon banked away to the right in a diving turn. The Eon was once again alone. The white machine had gone, its passing so swift that I had been unable to identify it.

In the still air, the Eon continued down towards the airfield. We joined the circuit over the woods at 800 feet and flew parallel to the concrete runway down there on the right, flew towards the hangar from which fluttered the tricolor flag of France.

Suddenly, the aircraft lurched upwards. The seat of my pants told me that we were in the grip of the most almighty thermal that we had ever encountered. The variometer hadn't yet reacted before we were in a tight turn to the right. The thermal thrust and surged and pushed and the Eon lifted up from over the woods and rose into an empty sky, a vast sky that promised height, peace, and that very precious state of being alone. Not loneliness, but just being alone in a boundless sky.

I sat there, lightly holding the stick, my feet clear of the rudder pedals except for an occasional gentle press by one foot or the other, watching the tilted horizon revolve. The unseen power in the thermal tilted a wing and tried to push the aircraft over – an incipient spin, yielding to a push of my left foot. I increased speed to 30 knots. The thrusting air lifted the Eon to 4700 feet where I was just able to peep over the top of the haze that cloaked the earth. Mile upon mile of sky led the eye to an unreachable softening of distance until the furthermost limits of vision marked only the beginning of the enormous span of a boundless yet finite universe. With a piercing stab of insight that lasted for only a fraction of a second I understood the meaning of "infinity". Then the inadequate human intellect clouded over and I vainly tried to recall that which a few seconds earlier had been so brilliantly obvious. Still there was a contentment in the air, a wordless experience of just being there, looking over the top of the earth's hazy blanket. If only I could rid myself of this encumbrance of machine, this structure of wood, fabric, cables, pulleys and brackets! If only I could step out of it and just be here in a state of naturalness with no artificial, no man-made aids to flight! Just be here in infinite contentment – God's gift to the cows, but not to striving, thinking, goal-oriented man. Dear God, the price of intellect, of free will, is sometimes too high!

Far below, another glider, white and tiny against the olive-green of the woodlands, entered the base of the thermal. Unwilling to share my thermal with the intruder I flew away, aimlessly, sometimes this way, sometimes that, slowly descending at an unhurried 25 knots to the warmer air, quietly remembering the vision of limitless distance that I had been privileged to see in the sky that is always neutral.

13

NO GOING BACK

Had I now really got parachuting out of my system? Was I truly happy as a glider pilot surrounded by this structure of cockpit, wings, instrument panel, pulleys, cranks and control cables? It certainly allowed me more time in the air than I had enjoyed in earlier days. But it lacked the excitement and exhilaration of a well-executed, forceful exit from the door of a military transport aeroplane into the turbulent, battering slipstream blasting back from the racing propellers as one leapt strongly outwards and then fell through the airy maelstrom into the quiet, tranquil air beneath and behind the aeroplane. It lacked the feeling of elation as one climbed out of the fuselage of the old Rapide biplane and stood on the lower wing, with the wind of the slipstream ruffling one's overall sleeves as one reached out to grasp the strut. It lacked the confident elegance of that gentle leap backwards off the wing into the embrace of the air. It lacked that feeling of detachment as one lay spreadeagled on the air, rotating in a smoothly controlled turn, seeming to be stationary in space with the earth a mile below rotating in obedience to one's command.

Perhaps one last visit to Netheravon? Finally to cut a mental static line? I had no intention of jumping again, but my full membership of the British Parachute Association was paid up to date, and I did have my parachuting log book with me. . . . I motored down there, made myself known to the staff and was booked in for the night.

In the hour before dusk the sun was a red disc behind the distant haze. On Salisbury Plain the first faint wisps of evening mist were filling the hollows and softening the distances. The wind had dropped to a mild breeze. There was a quietness over all. In that hour before dusk in late September, I stood quite still in the middle of Netheravon Airfield, saturating in the atmosphere of the place, reluctant to break the spell of the hour.

From this airfield more than half a century ago in the dawn of military aviation, young men of whom England was justly proud took to the air in fragile, unreliable, barely understood machines, learning the basic flying skills that would help them kill their country's enemies. Some of these youngsters died here at Netheravon. They died because of inadequate training or lack of skill. And sometimes, trapped in a blazing inferno of petrol-soaked flying suit and fiery fabric and wood, they welcomed the merciful stab of the fire-crew's boathook.

To the north were the new, modern buildings and hangars. But to the east and south, apart from one newish barn in the south-west corner of the airfield, I saw the same landscape as those early aviators. I saw the same slopes of the land, the same woods, the same sky. Nothing, it seemed, had changed. I was here on a pleasure visit, to shoot a few feet of film of modern young men parachuting. If only their predecessors of half a century before had had the benefit of parachutes!

As I stood there, I heard from over the rise of the airfield, but out of sight, the sound of the Rapide's motors at full throttle as it began its take-off run. Suddenly, with painful intensity, I wished more than anything else in the world that I could be in it, kitted up ready to parachute. I busied myself with my photographic exposure meter, measuring the intensity of the light, and the mood passed as quickly as it had come.

Moments later the Rapide was visible away to the north-east on a left-hand circuit, straining for height. It flew into the sun and then turned towards the centre of the airfield on a steady course. It made one pass at just over 2000 feet. I heard the engines throttled back. Then one tiny, black, spreadeagled body appeared in the wake of the machine followed immediately by a developing canopy. A few seconds later a second parachutist appeared and almost immediately, I heard the engines at full throttle again as the Rapide started on another and higher circuit. This time round it dropped three bodies, three tiny black crosses that hurtled down towards the airfield for five seconds and then halted abruptly, swinging under their canopies. Down they floated, experimenting with their control toggles, turning now this way, now that. As they drifted lower, I heard two of them calling to each other with strong, young voices. Happy voices. One by one they turned their canopies to face into wind and prepared to land. A youthful voice overhead shouted, "Mind your head." I glanced up and grinned, because to my more experienced eye the youthful caller would land at least a hundred yards away downwind.

Safely down, the parachutists roughly packed their parachutes and strode up the slope to the hangar. Two of them walked together, chatting in a quiet, arm's length intimacy that only men seem to be able to understand and enjoy. Minutes later another group of young men were in the air. As the light faded and late afternoon became dusk, I packed my camera and strolled slowly off the airfield.

That evening, apart from the barman, I was the only person in the Aviation Officers' Mess. I ate a solitary dinner beneath the high-ranking gaze of the portraits ranged around the walls of the dining room. At one end of the room, over the fire-place, was a portrait of Brigadier-General George Harvey Nicholson. At the other end of the room was a painting of HH Prince Maurice of Battenburg in Light Infantry dress uniform. As I ate my chicken and roast potatoes they stared down at me, Field Marshal HRH the Duke of

Gloucester, General Sir Richard Haking, Arthur 1st Duke of Wellington, and one unnamed portrait, haughty, noble, distant.

I finished my meal and, well-fortified with brandy, decided to stroll up to the airfield as it was a still, warm, balmy night. At the red and white barrier the Ministry of Defence policeman looked at me severely, scrutinised my pass and handed it back to me without a word. I strolled on up the slight incline, past the parachute school buildings which were in darkness, and onto the turf of the airfield. Glancing up, I located the Pole Star to use it as a reference for finding my way back, then I struck out across the airfield. In a couple of hundred yards the ground sloped downwards until the hangars were out of sight. Now there was silence: no aircraft noise, no sound of traffic, no bird calls, just the light sound of my own footfalls. I continued towards that same south-eastern corner of the field where a few years previously I had landed in a field containing inquisitive cows.

It was silent, it was peaceful. Was it like this at the beginning of our earth's creation before it was populated and man invented noise pollution? I stood there luxuriating in the blessed quiet and open space. The stars twinkled in the Netheravon sky, unreachable light-years away: the Plough, Cassiopeia, Orion, constellations virtually unchanged for thousands of years. They represented permanence outside our world of change, unreachable yet accessible on a quiet, clear night such as this when a parachutist turned glider pilot wanted peace, to be alone, to think.

I thought how splendid it would be to go back in time some twenty or thirty years, but armed with my present knowledge and experience. Would I have changed anything? Yes, many things! One thing I would not have changed would be coming to Netheravon, this haven, and learning the elementary skills of free-fall parachuting, that quest for perfection rarely to be achieved. Once, and only once, I made a perfect ten-second free-fall delay and opening. On that one occasion I knew that this was a faultless free-fall descent, even as I fell from 4400 feet through the cold, clear, crisp November air above Netheravon. It was the only time in my life that I have achieved perfection.

Tonight I am standing here in the middle of this quiet, empty airfield as the result of a decision taken years before when I strode into Seaforth Barracks and joined the TA. I still have no idea why I did it. Why submit to military discipline again? Why put up with discomfort again? All too easy to say, ''You must have been mad;'' But I wasn't. Tonight, standing there on Netheravon airfield I'm glad I did. It had nothing to do with Field Marshal Sir William Slim's ''Twice a citizen''. It had nothing to do with defending the country against the Russians or anyone else. I have no idea why I did it. But I'm glad I did. It was exciting, at times somewhat alarming, but overall very satisfying.

Netheravon at this time of night is silent. I am standing still in the middle of this grass airfield, listening. It is so quiet that when I move my head I can hear my neck muscles sliding over each other. Some night creature scuffles softly past me. I shiver although it is not cold. The spell is broken. I walk briskly back, guided by the star, until the hangars come into view, black against the faint glow of the night sky.

INDEX